The Letters of Sigmund Freud to Jeanne Lampl-de Groot, 1921–1939

I0028279

Freud wrote 76 letters to the Dutch psychoanalyst Jeanne Lampl-de Groot between 1921 and 1939. These letters are personable, lively, and compassionate and convey his respect and caring for Jeanne, who was his patient, pupil, and eventually his esteemed professional colleague. The letters are sociohistorical documents that contain Freud's thoughts about pertinent issues in psychoanalysis and the interwar sociopolitical situation in Vienna and Germany.

Jeanne Lampl-de Groot was an internationally known psychoanalyst who published extensively on psychoanalytic theory and practice. She regularly wrote long letters to Freud when residing outside of Vienna, seeking his advice on personal and professional matters and discussing with him her evolving ideas about psychoanalysis, including her disagreement with Freud about female sexual development. It is unfortunate that Jeanne had her letters to Freud destroyed because it sometimes makes Freud's somewhat elliptical responses difficult to place in context. For example, it is quite probable that she wrote detailed descriptions of her husband's emotional issues, which Freud then merely alluded to. Because we don't know the specifics of what she wrote, his responses remain ambiguous, and therefore problematic to translate. Nonetheless, Freud's responses do reveal a great deal about Jeanne and her passion for psychoanalysis. The book also includes several of her letters to her parents, which allows the reader to get to know Jeanne's intelligent, thoughtful voice, her thoughts about the evolving science of psychoanalysis, her experience during her psychoanalysis with Freud, and her concerns about the rise of anti-Semitism in Austria and Germany.

This book introduces to its readers a very personable Freud and provides insight into his thoughts about the development of critical psychoanalytic concepts such as the death drive, masochism, lay analysis, and his changing views on the length of a psychoanalysis. We also hear about historical events in the 1920s and 1930s as we witness Freud and Lampl-de Groot move through their personal and professional lives with dignity and perseverance.

Gertie Bögels is a former psychiatrist at the Nijmegen University Medical Center and former co-editor of the Dutch *Tijdschrift voor Psychoanalyse*. Her publications include works on biography and psychoanalysis, narrative and imagination, child analysis, and intergenerational symptomatology.

The International Psychoanalytical Association
International Psychoanalysis Library Series
Series Editor: Silvia Flechner
IPA Publications Committee
Fred Busch, Natacha Delgado, Nergis Güleç, Thomas
Marcacci, Carlos Moguillansky, Rafael Mondrzak, Angela M.
Vuotto, Gabriela Legoretta (consultant)

"Gertie Bögels makes accessible 76 carefully annotated letters written by Sigmund Freud to Jeanne Lampl-de Groot between 1921 and 1939. They show him as a colleague, a helper, a scientist, and a critical observer of the current political situation. Unfortunately, Lampl-de Groot had her letters to Freud destroyed. Nonetheless, the book deftly places her personality and the details of her life in historical context, and the reader will get to know her as a young woman making a place for female identity, not only in psychoanalytic theory but also as an active participant in the political debates within the international psychoanalytic movement of the time."

– Stephan Hau (Psychoanalyst, IPA), professor for clinical psychology, Department of Psychology, Stockholm University

"What a beautiful book! It introduces us to an elderly Freud captivated by a young, ambitious Dutch woman who becomes a noted analyst and one of his confidantes. I was particularly impressed by Freud's creativity and grandfatherly cordiality as he works tirelessly on into old age while bearing the pain and complications of his cancer with dignity."

– Marc Hebbrecht, MD, psychiatrist, training analyst of the Belgian Society of Psychoanalysis

"Over his lifetime, Sigmund Freud wrote thousands of letters to important contemporaries, colleagues, and friends, including more than 70 letters to Jeanne Lampl-de Groot. These letters give us a vivid glimpse into his relationship with a promising young doctor, who later became a close friend of the Freud family, and a female Nestor of the Dutch Psychoanalytic Society. The letters also reflect the cultural and political upheavals that marked the interwar years."

– Suzy Schipper, psychoanalyst; clinical psychologist; member, Dutch Psychoanalytic Society

"Bögels' beautifully and expertly edited and annotated book *Sigmund Freud: Letters to Jeanne Lampl-de Groot 1921–1939* presents for the first time Sigmund Freud's correspondence between 1921 and 1939 with the renowned Dutch psychoanalyst Jeanne Lampl-de Groot. This major contribution to the psychoanalytic literature shows a personable, supportive, and deeply engaged Freud, who as Jeanne's psychoanalyst, friend, and mentor also provides astute commentary on psychoanalytic developments and societal issues, including the rising Austrian/German anti-Semitism. Additionally, Bögels introduces Jeanne Lampl-de Groot through her intelligent, passionate letters to her parents, and we learn how her innovative conceptions on female psychosexual development influenced Freud."

– Rita Teusch, Ph.D. training and supervising psychoanalyst, Boston Psychoanalytic Society and Institute

The Letters of Sigmund Freud to Jeanne Lampl-de Groot, 1921–1939

Psychoanalysis and Politics in the Interwar Years

Edited by Gertie Bögels

Translated by Kenneth Kronenberg

Routledge
Taylor & Francis Group

LONDON AND NEW YORK

Cover image: E. & R. Berkovits-Lampl Archive

First published in English 2023
by Routledge
4 Park Square, Milton Park, Abingdon, Oxon OX14 4RN

and by Routledge
605 Third Avenue, New York, NY 10158

Routledge is an imprint of the Taylor & Francis Group, an informa business

English translation by Kenneth Kronenberg

First published in The Netherlands as *Sigmund Freud: Brieven aan Jeanne Lampl-de Groot. 1921–1939*. Redactie, inleiding en vertaling Gertie Bögels © Uitgeverij Sjibbolet, Amsterdam, 2012.

ISBN 978-94-9111-007-8

The translation is based on the German edition of the book: *Sigmund Freud. Briefe an Jeanne Lampl-de Groot 1921–1939*. By Gertie Bögels in collaboration with Joachim F. Danckwardt. Transcription by Gerhard Fichtner.

Gießen: Psychosozial-Verlag © 2017

Psychosozial-Verlag, www.psychosozial-verlag.de

ISBN 978-3-8379-2568-5

Illustrations: E. & R. Berkovits-Lampl Archive, unless otherwise indicated

The English translation was made possible by financial support from the Stichting Psychoanalytische Fondsen, Amsterdam, and the DPV-Stiftung, Berlin

British Library Cataloguing-in-Publication Data
A catalogue record for this book is available from the British Library

Library of Congress Cataloging-in-Publication Data
A catalog record for this book has been requested

ISBN: 978-1-032-21382-8 (hbk)
ISBN: 978-1-032-21381-1 (pbk)
ISBN: 978-1-003-26813-0 (ebk)

DOI: 10.4324/9781003268130

Typeset in Palatino
by Apex CoVantage, LLC

For Edith and Robert Berkovits-Lampl, in friendship

Contents

Series Editor's Foreword

The Letters of Sigmund Freud to Jeanne Lampl-de Groot, 1921–1939: Psychoanalysis and Politics in the Interwar Years

The Publications Committee of the International Psychoanalytic Association continues the series "Psychoanalytic Ideas and Applications" with the present volume.

The aim of this series is to focus on the production of significant authors, whose works are outstanding contributions to the development of the psychoanalytic field, and to set out relevant ideas and themes generated by psychoanalysis throughout its history that deserve to be known and discussed by present day psychoanalysts.

The relationship between psychoanalytic ideas and their applications needs to be highlighted from the perspective of theory, clinical practice, and research in order to maintain their validity for contemporary psychoanalysis.

The Publications Committee's objective is to share these ideas with the psychoanalytic community and with professionals in other related disciplines so as to expand their knowledge and generate a productive interchange between the text and the reader.

The IPA Publications Committee is pleased to publish the English translation of *The Letters of Sigmund Freud to Jeanne Lampl-de Groot, 1921–1939: Psychoanalysis and Politics in the Interwar Years,* by Gertie Bögels. The present volume is an expanded edition of a book published in 2012, in Dutch, in the Netherlands, and also published in 2017, in German. It contains 76 letters written by Freud between 1921 and 1939 to the well-known Dutch psychoanalyst Jeanne Lampl-de Groot.

Dr. Bögels was close to Lampl-de Groot, who in fact was her supervisor during her analytic training. Her appreciation for Lampl-de Groot led her to invest considerable time and energy to obtain the letters and find additional information regarding her personal and family life. Dr. Bögels requested Freud's letters from the Library of Congress in 2009. This volume makes the 76 letters written by Freud to Lampl-de Groot available in English for the first time. Unfortunately, Lampl-de Groot's letters to Freud were destroyed by Anna Freud at her request.

Dr. Bögels' book begins with biographical information about Jeanne Lampl-de Groot. The richness of her description poignantly brings her character alive. One learns of the death of two sisters and the long mourning process that marked her life. We learn about her great interest in music and literature, her passion for psychoanalysis, and her substantial contributions to psychoanalytic theory. Lampl-de Groot's work focused on Freud's theory of the sexual development of women, paying particular attention to the role of the mother. She published several papers on this topic, one of the best known being "The Evolution of the Oedipus Complex in Women."

The second chapter, entitled "My Dear Jeanne," presents Freud's letters. Dr. Bögels' footnotes and comments, which greatly enrich those letters, include sociopolitical and biographical information about all of the persons and events mentioned in the letters, and provide a social, political, intellectual, and personal background to Freud's correspondence. In reading the letters, one is struck by Freud's evident affection and respect for his most gifted student and esteemed colleague. The letters convey personal exchanges and commentary about the development of psychoanalysis, and also about the rise of the Nazi regime and anti-Semitism, which eventually forced both Freud and Lampl-de Groot to flee. In this respect, the letters are a window into these difficult historical times.

Dr. Bögels' third chapter provides excerpts from letters that Lampl-de Groot wrote to her parents between 1921 and 1923, which evince a remarkable writing talent. They convey the quality of her relationship with her parents and her interest in sharing her experiences in Italy and Vienna with them. In the absence of her letters to Freud, these excerpts also give us insight into their relationship. They include references to the letters she received from Freud, including his response to her request to start psychoanalysis with him. She also told her parents about her first sessions with Freud and her impressions of him. Dr. Bögels skillfully chose excerpts from these letters that shed light on the development of psychoanalysis at that time, including theory, technique, training models, and psychoanalytic organizations. These fragments enable the reader to appreciate the milieu, and the conditions in which psychoanalytic life developed.

This book is an important contribution to understanding Freud's relationship to Lampl-de Groot, and more generally to the history of the psychoanalytic movement, and to the struggles it faced during those most difficult years in Europe. It is a testament to the meaningful contributions that Jeanne Lampl-de Groot made to psychoanalysis. We are indebted to Dr. Bögels and to the translator Kenneth Kronenberg for making this exceptional volume available to an English-speaking readership.

Gabriela Legorreta
Series Editor
Chair, IPA Publications Committee

Introduction

Introduction

> "a small piece of emigrant misery beside the large."

The article "Freud als Briefschreiber" [Freud as letter writer] in *Jahrbuch der Psychoanalyse* begins with this quotation from a letter from Sigmund Freud, the founder of psychoanalysis, to Jeanne Lampl-de Groot, Freud's last analysand. She went on to become an internationally recognized psychoanalyst and the Nestor of Dutch psychoanalysis. But in 1938 both of them had had to flee Nazi terror in Vienna. Freud had taken his family to London; Lampl-de Groot, her children, and her Jewish husband Hans Lampl made their way to the home of her parents in The Hague. The author of that article, Gerhard Fichtner, held a chair in the History of Medicine, at Tübingen University, where his research specialty was the history of psychiatry and psychoanalysis. He was the editor of numerous collections of Freud letters and co-edited the "bridal letters" (*Brautbriefe*) from Freud to his future wife, Martha Bernays. That 1938 letter to Lampl-de Groot demonstrates Freud's ability to portray one of the most dramatic periods in world history from the perspective of his family's current situation, an example of social history *avant la lettre*. It is well known that Freud wrote thousands of letters, including the above-cited bridal letters, to colleagues and prominent contemporary authors such as Karl Abraham, Eugen Bleuler, Max Eitingon, Carl Jung, the Greek princess Marie Bonaparte, Arnold and Stefan Zweig, Lou Andreas-Salomé, and Thomas Mann.

Once it became clear to me from this Freud letter's reception that there must be other letters to Lampl-de Groot, in 2009 I ordered a copy of this correspondence from the Library of Congress, in Washington, D.C. The trove consisted of 76 letters, although access to two of them had been restricted until 2008. I also found that the letters were written in Sütterlin, the old German script, which I found difficult to decipher. Thanks to Joachim Danckwardt, I made contact with Fichtner, who offered to transcribe them

DOI: 10.4324/9781003268130-1

for me on the condition that I cite him in future publications. Until his death, on January 4, 2012, he was very helpful to me in elucidating unclear passages and Austrian colloquialisms. Only once was I able to correct an error of his: it related to the word *Selecta*, which Fichtner had thought was the name of a medical journal. My own Internet research identified it as a brand of cigars. Fichtner was quite amused: how could he have missed that one! After all, cigars were a recurrent preoccupation of Freud's, and the delivery of Dutch cigars came up frequently in his correspondence with the Lampls.

Jeanne's daughter Edith Berkovits-Lampl and her son-in-law Robert Berkovits generously provided me with further information and correspondences. Among other things, they had a copy of the numbered list of the Freud letters and several short notes handwritten by Jeanne Lampl. The list was prepared on November 8, 1986, in London, on the occasion of Jeanne Lampl's official handover of the 76 letters and postcards to the then president and vice president of the International Psychoanalytical Association, Robert Wallerstein and Joseph Sandler. The transfer was witnessed by the American psychoanalyst Charles Mangham.[1]

Edith Berkovits-Lampl was able to obtain information about the two restricted letters from the Freud archive in Washington even before 2008. They were thus able to gain access to them despite the restriction; however, they contained nothing of particular interest, a circumstance well known from other archived correspondences.[2]

---

1 The original letters are housed in the Library of Congress, in Washington DC, in the following collection:

   SIGMUND FREUD, GENERAL CORRESPONDENCE
   Box 36 Folder 4 (Lampl-de Groot, Jeanne 1921–1925)
   Box 36 Folder 5 (Lampl-de Groot, Jeanne 1926–1929)
   Box 36 Folder 6 (Lampl-de Groot, Jeanne 1931)
   Box 36 Folder 9 (Lampl-de Groot, Jeanne 1932, Jan – May)
   Box 36 Folder 7 (Lampl-de Groot, Jeanne 1932, June – Dec)
   Box 36 Folder 8 (Lampl-de Groot, Jeanne 1933)
   Box 36 Folder 10 (Lampl-de Groot, Jeanne 1937 – 1938)
   Box 36 Folder 2 (Lampl, Hans + Lampl-de Groot, Jeanne 1938 – 1939)

2 Edith Berkovits was surprised that the library had looked at the letters even though they were restricted. The then curator of the Sigmund Freud collection, Science Manuscript Specialist Dr. Leonard C. Bruno, responded to my query about whether the restriction actually concerned these two letters in particular:
      The two letters from Freud (Dec. 29, 1938 & Apr. 3, 1939) came with other material to the Library in 1960 from Dr. Kurt Eissler, Sigmund Freud Archives (the source of much of our Freud holdings) and it was restricted by the donor. It would have been unusual if Dr. Eissler had not placed some restriction on the donation, as it seems to have been his practice to err on the side of extreme caution. Although the letters in question were closed until 2008, in fact, the Library vetted them for patient names some time before that and, per its usual policy, made copies and placed them in the open part of the

As far as the letters from Jeanne to Freud are concerned, these were destroyed by Anna Freud at Jeanne's request. In a letter to Jeanne dated December 31, 1939, Anna Freud noted from London: "I immediately looked for and destroyed your letters because I know that this is what you wanted."

It should be noted that letters or texts in a decedent's estate are frequently saved despite the author's expressed desire. We can only guess why Anna Freud complied with Jeanne's request.

The Berkovits-Lampl archive from the period of the Freud-Lampl letters also contains a photograph of Dr. Wagner-Jauregg, the professor of neuropsychiatry in Vienna, under whom Jeanne received her psychiatric training at the same time as her psychoanalytic. The handwritten dedication reads: "To Dr. De Groot for assistance rendered. Vienna June 6, 1924, Wagner-Jauregg."[3]

Gertie Bögels, Maarn, The Netherlands 2022

---

collection (leaving the originals in the closed section until their open date was reached). Presently, there are no longer any Lampl de Groot materials in the Freud papers that are not open, so you have received all there is. I can understand your puzzlement as to why the letters were ever closed, and your reaction is that of many a researcher who, upon finally gaining access to something previously restricted in the Freud papers, finds they are often disappointed or at least underwhelmed.

3 "Frau Dr. De Groot für geleistete Hülfe. Wien 6/VI 1924 Wagner-Jauregg"

Jeanne Lampl-de Groot
October 16, 1895 to April 4, 1987

Biographical notes

Jeanne (Adriana) Lampl-de Groot often made a point of noting that she had been analyzed by Freud. The extent to which this determined her life and her position in the psychoanalytic movement became manifest through her correspondence with Freud conducted over a period of almost 20 years. More than 70 letters from that correspondence written by Freud are now being made available in English for the first time.

Jeanne Lampl had been raised in a cosmopolitan and humanistic atmosphere. Her family, which had acquired considerable wealth, loved the arts, played music, and was socially engaged. Her mother, Henriëtte Dupont (1864–1951), was the daughter of a physician in Rotterdam. Jeanne's father, Michael Coenradus Mari de Groot (1860–1935), was the eighth of 13 children of a Catholic distiller, who later became a commission agent in the alcohol industry. In a memorial dedicated to him, he was described as engaged in city politics and having a nonconformist personality.[1] Over the course of his life, he rid himself of dogmatic religious beliefs and became increasingly engaged around social issues, especially relating to the "development of the working class." At about the time Jeanne was born he founded the Volkshaus, where general education courses, lectures, and musical performances were held. A few years later, he provided the financial means for founding a local public library. He became heavily involved in organizing various interest groups to address the impoverishment resulting from the closure of small distilleries.[2] One of her father's brothers was a professor of sinology at the University of Leiden, prior to that a professor in Berlin.

Jeanne was born in Schiedam on October 16, 1895, the third of four daughters: Jo, who was four and a half years older; Miek, two years

---

1 Kedde, B. (1972). *Herinneringen aan een groot Schiedammer* [Recollections of a Great Schiedammer]. Schiedam: Drukkerij de Eendracht.
2 According to the newspaper *Schiedamsche Courant*, 1891–1917. See http://scyedam. delinea.nl/kaleida/pagina.php?id=221 (last accessed May 9, 2021).

DOI: 10.4324/9781003268130-2

older; and Henriëtte, three and a half years younger. Her younger sister died of meningitis when Jeanne was just six years old, and shock at the sudden death and her mother's subsequent depression were to have lasting effects on her later development. When she was 80, Jeanne was finally able to describe in one of her last articles the experience of mourning in a girl she called Mary. In this anonymized medical case history, titled "Mourning in a 6-Year-Old Girl,"[3] she explained that it was based on childhood memories and reconstructions of events that emerged during the psychoanalysis of an adult. It is interesting that she tried to hide the fact that she was writing about herself. I once asked her whether it wasn't about her. A bit shocked, she responded, "How do you know?" When I explained that I felt it was written with such unusual empathy, she admitted it.

In interviews, she repeatedly stressed that she herself underwent analysis for professional reasons, and that she was a physically healthy and active person. On the other hand, she intimated that she had suffered frequent periods of depression, which, however, impeded neither her studies nor her work. Her letters to her parents, however, convey a somewhat different picture. When she was 26, shortly before beginning her psychoanalysis with Freud, Jeanne signed one of her letters from Italy to her mother as "Your youngest," thereby perhaps unconsciously acknowledging the reality of her sister's death and assuming her sister's place in the birth order. Or she may perhaps have denied this childhood trauma after the fact. It may also have been a factor in her decision to change her birth name from Adriana to Jeanne, the name of her favorite maternal aunt, possibly because this aunt had been more emotionally present for her. The fact that Freud had experienced a similar death, namely that of his one-year younger brother Julius, when Freud was two, may well have contributed to a sense of connection. Freud noted just such psychological connections in *The Interpretation of Dreams*, which Jeanne had read in 1913.[4]

Jeanne's interest in psychoanalysis developed during a period in which a network of interested physicians and nonphysicians was forming in the Netherlands, specifically in the area around Leiden and The Hague. In February 1914 Gerbrandus Jelgersma (1859–1942), since 1899 the first holder of the teaching chair in psychiatry in the Netherlands, held his rectorate address titled "Unconscious Mental Life" on the occasion of the 339th anniversary of the founding of the University of Leiden. In his official capacity, he recognized the incalculable value of Freud's studies

3 Lampl-de Groot, J. (1976). "Mourning in a 6-Year-Old Girl." *Psychoanalytic Study of the Child*, 31, 273–281.
4 Freud, S. (1900 [1953]). "The Interpretation of Dreams." In *Standard Edition of the Complete Psychological Works of Sigmund Freud*, vols. IV and V. London: Hogarth Press.

for the diagnosis and treatment of psychiatric conditions. Jelgersma thus became the first academic advocate of psychoanalysis. But at home there was an easier way for Jeanne to find information about psychoanalysis. In the spring of 1914, her oldest sister wrote a letter to Freud as a member of the board of her medical student association, inviting him to lecture. The outbreak of World War I made this lecture impossible. Later, however, Jeanne read her sister's letter, as she told an interviewer in 1980.[5] She had read *The Interpretation of Dreams* when she was 18 and had been completely captivated. She began her medical studies in Leiden, later continuing them in Amsterdam because Leiden was too "sleepy" for her. She missed the museums and concerts.

In January 1917, when Jeanne turned 21, her oldest sister Jo, who had been very important to her, died of pneumonia. Jo and her fiancé – both physicians – had traveled to Paris to help the Red Cross care for war casualties; it was to have been an opportunity to gain valuable medical experience. The loss of Jo, who had served as a role model in her choice to study medicine and psychoanalysis, undoubtedly compounded Jeanne's depression brought on by the previous loss of her youngest sister. After completing her medical training, Jeanne and a girlfriend traveled to Italy. She herself viewed this as freedom regained after the isolation of World War I, during which the Netherlands had remained "neutral." Such travels would have been virtually impossible during those years. But one can also interpret Jeanne's trip to Italy as a flight from her parents' house during this second period of mourning: Italy, the warm, colorful representation of a picture book from her childhood, which she described in her study "Mourning in a 6-Year-Old Girl."

In addition to musicmaking, her parents had also stressed writing and reading. This is evident from Jeanne's intensive correspondence with her mother during her trip to Italy, as well as before she began her psychoanalysis with Freud, and continuing in Vienna. In her letters to her mother, she included theoretical reflections on psychoanalysis and described – understandably only in summary – her intimate personal experiences. She introduced her mother to the professional literature so that she could get a better picture of the training that so fascinated her daughter. At the same time, she cited parts of the new psychoanalytical theory, according to which fixation on mourning is viewed as a highly personal narcissistic satisfaction. Music was a recurrent topic, especially Beethoven's piano sonatas, which mother and daughter had practiced together, and it appears to have been connected with a preverbal, unexpressed experience of mourning. Only over the course of psychoanalysis, during which the memorialization of death dates became a recurrent

5   Video of a conversation with training candidates at the Psychoanalytic Institute in Amsterdam, September 1980.

theme, did she find the words to relate her loss to her parents. Bach's "*St. Matthew Passion*" and Mahler's "Songs on the Death of Children" were crucial in enabling them to go through the process of mourning together.

In her first letter to Freud, in the summer of 1921, Jeanne wrote that she intended to travel through Italy first. Freud wrote back immediately, as was his habit, not in Latin script, but in Sütterlin, addressing her as "Sehr geehrtes Fräulein Doktor." That he concluded the letter with "With best wishes and a little envy," was a revelation to her: the fact that one could simply be envious and openly express that envy at the same time! This naïve "unconscious" test of strength on the part of a 25-year-old physician who had just been certified, and who was the same age as Freud's youngest daughter, Anna, may have amused him and made him curious. For Jeanne it was probably a triumph of self-assertion when she later wrote Freud from Italy that she wished to postpone the start of analysis and extend her stay in Italy a few months longer because of the riots that were taking place in Vienna at the time. Although this request might have seemed acceptable, it may just have been an excuse. Or did she perhaps fear the start of analysis, even for "professional reasons"? In any event, Freud replied that a later starting date was better for him as well. Jeanne was 26 years old when she began psychoanalysis in the spring of 1922, the same year in which Anna Freud gained entry to the Vienna Psychoanalytic Society, after presenting her paper titled "Beating Fantasies and Daydreams." Jeanne had attended the reading and wrote her mother about it enthusiastically. The two women got to know each other at scientific events at the Society and became intimate friends, a friendship that lasted for the rest of their lives.

In addition to her analysis, which took place six times a week in sessions lasting 55 minutes, Jeanne also attended evening classes. She immersed herself in the psychoanalytic literature and after some time was permitted to begin a supervised analysis. Her first patient was an acquaintance from the Netherlands who had been in analysis with Johan van Ophuijsen[6] but later came to live in Vienna.[7]

Eduard Hitschmann, director of the Vienna Psychoanalytic Ambulatorium[8] in the Pelikangasse, referred two other patients to her as supervised cases. Because of the lack of space at the Institute – it was even closed temporarily by the health authorities – she treated patients in her own apartment, a situation that today's training candidates know well.

---

6 Johan H.W. van Ophuijsen was one of the most important advocates in the early days of psychoanalysis. Stroeken, H. (2009). "Johan van Ophuijsen, Padang/Indonesia 1882 – New York 1950." *Luzifer Amor*, 22, 7–44.

7 Groen-Prakken, H. & Ladan, A. (eds.). (1993). *The Dutch Annual of Psychoanalysis*, vol. I. Amsterdam: Swets & Zeitlinger, pp. 13f.

8 Founded in Vienna in May 1922, the Ambulatorium was the second psychoanalytic clinic after the one in Berlin, which had opened in February 1920.

In Vienna, Jeanne was confronted with anti-Semitism and anti-Semitic violence. Anti-Semitism became a topic of discussion in her psychoanalysis; she cited Freud as saying that everyone is infected with anti-Semitism but that he could find no evidence for it in her. In her conversation with training candidates, Jeanne named the men who – apart from her father – had played an important role in her development. Only later did she realize that all of them had been of Jewish ancestry. The first was the Jewish director of her middle school, with whom she had had a good relationship as a student. Then there was the older Jewish painter J.J. Isaäcson,[9] who had allowed her to study in his atelier while she was in medical school, a time when she had suffered from depression. Jeanne continued to correspond with Isaäcson even from Italy. The third was Freud. It is noteworthy that in the 1980 interview cited earlier, she did not mention another Jewish man in her life, namely her husband Hans Lampl, who had died in 1958. He had been killed in a car accident on a day on which the streets had been unexpectedly icy, and Jeanne had lost control of the automobile. She slammed into a tree, and he died instantly; she sustained serious leg and pelvic fractures. After surgery, she had to be taken care of for months, a task that Edith and Robert Berkovits-Lampl and their children lovingly took upon themselves.

In 1922 she took her neurology and psychiatry training in Vienna under Prof. Julius Wagner-Jauregg, a student contemporary of Freud's and one of the few with whom Freud was on a familiar "Du" basis.[10] He, however, had little interest in psychoanalysis. In September 1922 she attended the 7th International Psychoanalytic Congress in Berlin – the last one that Freud was able to attend. From a scientific perspective, it was an important congress in that it marked the beginning of ego psychology. Sándor Ferenczi, Karl Abraham, Melanie Klein, and Karen Horney presented papers. It was at these meetings that she got to know her future husband, Hans Lampl. Freud supposedly told him in a letter that a "young Dutch woman" would be attending the congress and asked whether he might look after her a bit.[11] At the time, Lampl was working as a psychoanalyst at the Berlin Institute. He knew Freud's son Martin from his school days and was a friend of the family. He had been mentioned in one of Freud's letters to his daughter Anna as early as July 7, 1908. In this letter he mentioned that Lampl would

9   Joseph Jacob Isaäcson, born April 20, 1859, was a well-known painter. Originally from The Hague, he lived in Paris and later in Amsterdam. In October 1942, at the age of 83, he and his wife were taken to the transit camp at Westerbork, from where they were deported to Auschwitz. Isaäcson was murdered there on December 12, 1942.

10 Julius Wagner-Jauregg (1857–1940) was an Austrian physician and psychiatrist who was awarded the Nobel Prize in Physiology and Medicine in 1927. Toward the end of his life he was known to be anti-Semitic and a believer in eugenics and racial hygiene. He opposed giving women the vote. He supported the Nazi party, at least after the annexation of Austria in 1938, and applied for party membership. It is not known whether his "cynicism" about psychoanalysis that Jeanne Lampl described in a letter to her parents on February 5, 1923 may have been a manifestation of anti-Semitism.

11 Oral communication from Edith Berkovits-Lampl in 2012.

accompany Martin to Dietfeldhof, the house in Berchtesgaden where the family vacationed.[12] In contrast to Freud's sons, Hans, like Freud, became a passionate cigar smoker; Freud's last brief note to Lampl from the year 1938 contains references to a particular brand of cigars and the preferred shape.

Freud was almost 67 years old when, in February 1923, he self-diagnosed leukoplakia, a precursor of cancer, in his gums and right upper jaw. He had surgery two months later, on April 20, after which he suffered profuse bleeding. Only then did he tell Ernest Jones, because he was not in the habit of discussing his health with others, with the exception of Ferenczi.[13] On the other hand, in his correspondence with Jeanne during the following years, he consistently made reference to his health and to radiation or other surgery that he was forced to undergo. In a letter to her parents, dated April 26, 1923, Jeanne wrote about Freud's jaw surgery, and about the resultant bleeding, as well as about her fears and worries. She subsequently reported on April 30 that "Prof. Freud began again this morning and says that he is feeling very well." This would not have sounded particularly convincing, and it is perhaps significant that she apparently wrote no further letters to her parents.

Jeanne celebrated Christmas at her parents' home in The Hague in 1924. She moved to Berlin in February 1925, where she continued her training at the Psychoanalytic Ambulatorium. It is clear from the address on one of Freud's letters that a relationship between Jeanne and Hans Lampl must already have existed in March 1925: "Dr. H. Lampl for Dr. J. De Groot, Berlin, Blumeshof 16." Jeanne's parents met their future son-in-law in the Hague for the first time on the day before the wedding, on April 7, 1925. The couple announced their new status to Freud in a telegram: "Verein zu Zweit geschlossen" [Pair association entered into/closed]. Freud, responding to the ambiguity of the German word *geschlossen*, which can mean both "entered into" and "closed," responded, "I hope that it doesn't remain just a pair."[14] This wordplay regarding children came to have added meaning over the course of their correspondence, as Jeanne regularly discussed her worries about her husband's mood swings.

The Dutch Society, too, had sent Jeanne congratulations, as the following letter makes clear. On April 10, 1925, Jeanne, who was staying with Hans at the Hotel de L'Europe, in Amsterdam, wrote a letter to the secretary of the Society: "Dear colleague, in response to your letter of April 7, I hereby inform you that I wish to join the Dutch Psychoanalytical Society. At the same time I thank you for your congratulations. Greetings, Jeanne Lampl-De Groot."[15]

12 Freud, S. (1960). *Briefe 1873–1939*. Selected and edited by Ernst and Lucie Freud. Frankfurt a. M.: Fischer, p. 289.

13 Jones, E. (1957). *The Life and Work of Sigmund Freud*, vol. 3, 1st edition. New York: Basic Books, p. 89.

14 Oral communication from Edith Berkovits-Lampl, 2011.

15 Archive of the Dutch Psychoanalytical Association in the De Bazel City Archive, Amsterdam.

However, she terminated her membership in the Dutch Society on November 10, 1926; at the time her daughter was about 9 months old:

> Dear colleague . . . I also wish to inform you that I am terminating my membership in the Dutch Psychoanalytical Society because my permanent residence is now in Berlin, and I am going to become a member of the Berlin Psychoanalytic Society. I will thus continue to be a member of the International Society. I request that you convey to the Dutch Society my sincere thanks for their hospitality, as well as my regret that this hospitality resulted in so little that was useful. If in the future I have the opportunity to express my gratitude with a personal contribution, I will gladly avail myself of it. With collegial greetings, J. Lampl.[16]

Her time in Berlin was one of great contrasts. The Lampls built an imposing house in a tree-shaded quarter of Berlin, a modern, cube-shaped villa with separate practice rooms based on a design by Freud's son Ernst, who was an architect.[17] It became a meeting place for friends and colleagues, as well as for the Freuds' children and grandchildren. It still exists, since World War II with a traditional gabled roof, and is known as the Villa Lampl. This is where the Lampls' children were born, Henriëtte on January 30, 1926, and Edith on May 23, 1928. This is also where Jeanne wrote her first scientific paper. That the one was closely connected with the other became evident in 1927 when, now an experienced mother, she began to revise Freud's theory of the development of girls, and in the process did work on the specific role of the mother. It became her best known and most frequently cited paper "The Evolution of the Oedipus Complex in Women." This time period coincided with the blossoming of the international psychoanalytic movement. Enthusiastic physicians and psychologists as well as laypeople from all over the world came to Berlin to immerse themselves in the techniques of this fascinating new discipline. At the same time, political threats and street terror were becoming ever more prevalent. As a result of growing anti-Semitism and the increasing threat of Nazi violence, Jeanne and her Jewish husband and children decided, on Freud's advice, to return to Vienna in July 1933. He did not think that the international community would allow Nazi Germany to annex Austria. This was a year in which a large number of Jewish psychoanalysts fled to other European countries or the United States, including

---

16 Archive of the Dutch Psychoanalytical Association in the De Bazel City Archive, Amsterdam.
17 Until 1927 the address was Str. 88, no. 2; after 1929 the name was changed to Schumacherplatz 2. Today the address is Waldmeisterstraße 2. The Mauritanian Embassy is currently located there (information from Dr. Regine Lockot, Berlin, 2011).

August Watermann and Theodor Reik, and in 1934 Max Levy-Suhl, all of whom relocated to the Netherlands. Karl Landauer, cofounder of the Psychoanalytic Institute at the Frankfurt Institute for Social Research, emigrated to Sweden when the Institute was shuttered by the Nazis in March 1933 and all its books confiscated.[18] At the urging of van Ophuij-sen, who had received his training in Berlin and was in training analysis with Karl Abraham,[19] Landauer relocated to the Netherlands because van Ophuijsen wanted him as a training analyst in the Dutch training pro-gram.[20] Like Jeanne 10 years later, Landauer had also undergone training analysis with Freud and had completed his specialization in psychiatry under Wagner-Jauregg. However, the reception given to Jewish German psychoanalysts was less friendly than van Ophuijsen had imagined. The smoldering dispute among the various psychoanalytic factions regarding recognition of membership and training of analysts burst into the open. The Jewish psychoanalyst Jaap Spanjaard (1913–1985) wrote a nuanced account of the complex interactions among the various more or less organ-ized little groups of professional peers, noting in passing, "One would have to be a sociologist to describe more precisely the growing influence of psychoanalysis in Holland."[21] The sociologist Christien Brinkgreve took up the gauntlet, and her *Psychoanalyse in Nederland* [Psychoanalysis in the Netherlands] appeared in 1984, a historical and sociological work in which she discussed the complex evolution of psychiatric and psychoanalytic professional groups.[22] Not long before, Ilse Bulhof had published *Freud en Nederland* [Freud and the Netherlands], which had placed psychoana-lysis in a literary and cultural-historical context.[23] Landauer gave one of the speeches on the occasion of Freud's 80th birthday, in 1936, which the Lampls and their two daughters attended.

Jeanne shared in the growing interest in the psychoanalytic treatment of children and adolescents. She had become acquainted with Melanie Klein, who had conducted the first child analyses starting in 1921, which she continued after her resettlement in London in 1926. Jeanne's friend and colleague Siegfried Bernfeld had opened a clinic for adolescents in the 1920s. In 1936 Anna Freud and her life partner Dorothy Burlingham

18 Landauer, K. (1991). *Theorie der Affekte und andere Schriften zur Ich-Organisation* [Theory of Affects and Other Writings]. Ed. H.-J. Rothe. Frankfurt a.M.: Fischer.
19 Bentinck van Schoonheten, A. (2015). *Karl Abraham Life and Work: A Biography*. London: Routledge.
20 Rothe, H.-J. (ed.). (1991). *Karl Landauer: Theorie der Affekte und andere Schriften zur Ich-Organisation*. Frankfurt a.M.: Fischer.
21 Spanjaard, J. & Mekking, R. (1976). "Psychoanalyse in den Niederlanden." In D. Eicke (ed.), *Die Psychologie des 20. Jahrhunderts,* vol. III. Zurich: Kindler, pp. 55–72.
22 Brinkgreve, C. (1984). *Psychoanalyse in Nederland. Een vestigingsstrijd* [Psychoanalysis in the Netherlands. A Foundational Dispute]. Amsterdam: De Arbeiderspers.
23 Bulhof, I. (1983). *Freud en Nederland. De interpretatie en invloed van zijn ideeën* [Freud and the Netherlands: The Interpretation and Influence of his Ideas]. Baarn: Ambo.

founded the Jackson Day Nursery in Vienna, for children of impoverished Viennese between the ages of one and three. It was financed by Burlingham and received further financing from the American Edith Jackson (1895–1977).[24] Jackson had been in training analysis with Freud and was trained in child analysis by Anna Freud. She later returned to the United States. In Vienna, Jeanne accepted children for psychoanalysis "with half-board," because treatment could begin only after the hungry children had been given bread and butter and a glass of chocolate milk. However, this institution also closed after only two years because of the forced emigration of its staff. Shortly thereafter, similar reception camps were set up in London, the so-called War Nurseries, for children who had lost their parents as a result of Luftwaffe bombing raids. These later developed into the Hampstead Clinic, now the Anna Freud Centre, a renowned center for psychoanalytic treatment, training, and research.

In late March 1938, at the same time as the forced emigration of the Freud family, which had been able to travel by train through Germany via Paris to London with the help of Marie Bonaparte, Ernest Jones, and the American diplomat William C. Bullitt,[25] the Lampl family fled to Holland, leaving all of their possessions behind.[26] Until her house in the Haring-vlietstraat in Amsterdam was set up, the family lived at Belvédèreweg 11, in The Hague, with Jeanne's mother. Hans Lampl's mother took up residence in that house later. After Jeanne's arrival in the Netherlands, it was difficult for her to obtain Dutch citizenship. This was because her husband was Austrian, and she had lost her Dutch citizenship when Austria was annexed by Nazi Germany, making her and Hans unwilling German citizens. Marie Bonaparte interceded with Dutch princess Juliana, and permission was eventually granted, "a very sad case," as Juliana wrote to Bonaparte.[27] This continued to be a problem in the immediate aftermath of the war; the Lampls were not granted Dutch citizenship until January 1949.

24 Young-Bruehl, E. (1988). *Anna Freud. A Biography*. New York: Summit Books, pp. 218–220.
25 William Christian Bullitt (1891–1967) was an American journalist and diplomat. In 1933 President Roosevelt named him the first American ambassador to the Soviet Union (1933–1936); in 1936 Bullitt represented the United States in France. He negotiated the terms of Freud's emigration to London by way of Paris. The two knew each other well, as Bullitt had been in analysis with Freud in the 1920s.
26 Edith Berkovits-Lampl reported that the neighbors later told her that the apartment was immediately emptied, and when they asked where everything was taken, they were given the address of the SS. Nonetheless, she had positive memories of Vienna: how she and her mother went to the opera together; a performance of Mozart's "Magic Flute" with Richard Tauber and Lotte Lehmann; reading together with Jeanne in German because at the time the children spoke not a word of Dutch. She remembered how shocked she was when from one day to the next swastika flags were hung throughout the city.
27 Stouten, H. (2011). *Marie Bonaparte 1882–1962*. Amsterdam: Amsterdam University Press, pp. 167–171.

There are also letters from that time that make clear that Jeanne had unsuccessfully put out feelers about possible emigration to the United States, among others a very urgent request on May 17, 1940, a week after the Nazis invaded the Netherlands.

But in the meantime, Jeanne had quickly achieved a prominent role in Dutch psychiatric and psychoanalytic circles. She received invitations to lecture, and her advice was sought in the treatment of patients and the selection of training candidates. Differences of opinion began to emerge, although it became clear that Jeanne, with her more extensive experience at the training institutes in Vienna and Berlin, was the one who could best implement the internationally recognized training program in the Netherlands. Previous attempts by van Ophuijsen, and later by Landauer, to introduce this program failed because of differences of opinion with the less trained Dutch members. The licenses to practice of physicians who had immigrated were not recognized in Holland. The same issues that to this day can lead to controversies and splits in the psychoanalytic associations played a role even then: the obligatory training analysis, frequency of treatment, university degree requirements, and recognition as training analysts. As painful as it may be to imagine, anti-Semitism always seems to play a role in these controversies.

In addition to her organizational and training activities, she took a lead role in publishing Freud's texts. Among other things, she corresponded with Martin Freud for the translation rights; he wrote back in his father's name that although there was no one to whom he would rather grant publication rights, it would be better from a legal and practical perspective if the publisher would contact him directly, because various translation rights had already been granted to other publishers. However, he would leave the selection and organization of the material to her.[28] Discord erupted over translation rights as well: in an undated copy of a letter in response to a letter from the publisher Hollandia Drukkerij N.V., in Baarn, dated October 11, 1939, Martin wrote, "I wrote directly to Mrs. Lampl and hope to hear from her soon. May I make you aware that after the death of my father I own the translation rights in accordance with his provisions." However, Martin's distrust of the publisher grew. On November 15, 1939, he wrote Jeanne, "You see what they are. Swindlers." But in the end, he agreed with her:

> In case you haven't given up your idea of continuing with them, tell them that they must pay 120 h. fl.[29] for the translation rights, and that no counteroffer will be considered. But it would be a good idea if more

---

28 From the correspondence between Jeanne Lampl and Martin Freud, July 4 and July 11, 1939 (Edith Berkovits-Lampl Archive).

29 I.e., Dutch guilders.

of my father's work were translated into Dutch; a few translations have already appeared, but it seems to me they are of less important works. You would be doing me a great favor if you and your colleagues could find out which translations already exist.

The final sentence reads: "You know that all of my files and documents were destroyed."[30] In March 1936 the Gestapo had confiscated all of the Verlag's property,[31] including books from the German-Austrian book warehouse in Leipzig. On May 5, 1936, on the eve of Freud's 80th birthday, Ernest Jones inaugurated the new quarters of the "very mutilated torso" of the Verlag in Vienna, at Berggasse 7, close to Freud's home. The library and polyclinic were also located there; meetings were held there as well. As Jones wrote, "So, thanks to Martin Freud's energy, the Verlag managed to function until the Nazis confiscated it in March, 1938."[32]

After the Nazi invasion of Poland, on September 1, 1939, England declared war on Germany. Freud died less than a month later on the 23rd. His remains were cremated at Golder's Green Crematorium on September 26, as Jones reported, "in the presence of a large number of mourners, including Marie Bonaparte and the Lampls."[33] However, two condolence letters to Anna Freud, dated September 25, indicate that Hans and Jeanne Lampl-de Groot could not possibly have been present because they had been unable to get visas.[34] Jeanne wrote:

> My dear Anna, it is difficult for me to write to you now rather than simply spend a little time with you. But all of our attempts to get a visa have been completely unsuccessful; one is permitted to travel only when one represents state interests. Recently, I have often found myself thinking of Annenheim, which was also a difficult time for you. I had met you only shortly before, but I already knew that I would owe your father a debt of gratitude for everything good that promised to develop in my life. And later, as I was sleeping on the balcony at your place in Pötzleinsdorf and times were hard for me, I not only realized that your father was a physician and teacher to me, but had also become a friend and colleague [illegible], and that you too empathized with me. This was good for me, and I will never forget it. Perhaps it is silly to write something like that, but I felt a strong need to do so. Perhaps it will nonetheless be possible to [illegible] you in the

---

30 Letter from Martin Freud to Jeanne Lampl dated November 15, 1939 (ibid).

31 The Internationale Psychoanalytische Verlag, the private publishing house founded in 1919. It is often referred to simply as the Verlag.

32 Jones, E. (1957). Op. cit., p. 188.

33 Ibid., p. 246.

34 I am grateful to Yteke Hettinga, director of the Archive Committee of the Dutch Psychoanalytic Association, for this information.

near future. Now Hans and I can only think of you, and talk about you and about everything that was and is connected with you and your father. It is good in every respect that this is again possible. I hug you warmly, your Jeanne.[35]

And Hans Lampl wrote:

Dearest Anna! Yesterday was a Sunday that repeatedly reminded me of another Sunday many years ago. I arrived at the Berggasse and heard that Sophie[36] had died, and I came again in the evening and took a very long walk with you. And I was able to be together with you, as I often could in difficult times. And yesterday? I could do nothing other than think. Your father told me in Vienna, shortly before we left: this is no situation for you, you cannot bear a situation in which you are unable to do anything. And here it is again. I went to see the authorities today because I wanted to try to come to you. But travel is possible now only in the service of official interests. I had thought that it would work out, I even have your signature on a telegram: Anna Freud, a signature I imagine you thought might perhaps help me to come. All I can do, with Jeanne, is think intensely about you and know that you know. I sent a telegram to Stefi and asked her to inform your aunts.[37] It was thought that the travel regulations may soon be eased, and then I would come to you. It is very difficult not to be able to now, and so all I can do is send you greetings from afar, your Lampl.[38]

There is also a significant letter from Anna Freud to Jeanne, dated December 31, 1939:

Dear Jeanne! I'm sitting here on New Year's Eve, this time quietly at my desk; it would be difficult to say what there is to celebrate this time . . . What's going on in the outside world is mostly unpleasant. Jones is creating all kinds of difficulties regarding the plan for a complete English edition, which I very much want to come to fruition. I don't know yet whether it will happen. The situation with Dorothy hasn't changed at all. Although she has obtained permission to immigrate here, her emigration seems impossible.[39]

---

35 E. & R. Berkovits-Lampl archive.
36 Sophie Halberstadt-Freud (1893–1920) was Anna's older sister, the fifth of Freud's six children. She died of complications of the Spanish flu that was rampant in Europe in the interwar years.
37 According to the Sigmund Freud Museum Archive in Vienna, an Anna Stefanek looked after the Freud sisters there (signature 50/5).
38 E. & R. Berkovits-Lampl archive.
39 E. & R. Berkovits-Lampl archive.

After reporting on the well-being of family members, Anna continued:

> I immediately looked for and destroyed your letters because I know
> that this is what you wanted. It gave me an unpleasant feeling that
> personal letters from so many friends were stored down there. Now
> it's all been done.[40]

The destruction of this historically important material is unfortunate, as it
renders opaque some of Freud's responses to Jeanne. In some instances,
we can only guess at meanings.

At the beginning of the occupation, psychoanalysts in Holland continued to work as usual. After the decree that Jews could no longer be
members of a (in the language of the Nazis) "mixed" society, the members
collectively terminated their membership in the Dutch Psychoanalytical
Society, which was then officially dissolved. Jeanne and Hans's termina-
tions were dated October 28, 1941. Only the director and secretary continued in their official capacities in anticipation of the Society's revival.
Candidate training also continued underground. The poet Vasalis,[41] who
was in training at the time, wrote a dark depiction of the "hunger winter"
of 1944–1945, when people starved: "Twelve alien apostles around a circular table, form there a death-ride in the dark to a second house, and then a
technical course under a mercilessly shining lamp. All this without a sin-
gle drink, three hours long." Her training analysis was cut short on January 21, 1945, with the following entry in her diary: "At present, analysis is
at a standstill. No time and no desire." And: "Raids are expected day after
tomorrow."[42] Jaap Spanjaard described Landauer's influence on analytic
technique as a complete revision. Although there was considerable resistance at the beginning to the admission of Jewish German colleagues, he
noted that assimilation was now much less difficult as a result of Jeanne
and Hans's influence.[43]

The decrees promulgated by the occupying authorities became increasingly severe and far-reaching. Jewish physicians were no longer permitted to treat non-Jews, and in 1942 Jewish psychoanalysts were forced to
close their practices. Karl Landauer was arrested during a raid in 1943
and deported by way of the Westerbork transit camp to Bergen-Belsen,
where he died of starvation in January 1945. Hans Lampl was once forced

---

40 E. & R. Berkovits-Lampl archive.
41 The poet and psychiatrist M. Vasalis, pseudonym of Margaretha Droogleever Fortuyn-
    Leenmans (1909–1998). "Der Idiot im Bad" (1985). In M. Vasalis & G.A. van Oorschot
    (eds.), *Unbekannte Nähe. Moderne niederländische Lyrik bis 1980* [Unknown Closeness. Mod-
    ern Dutch Poetry to 1980]. Straelen: Straelener Manuskripte.
42 Meijer, M. (2011). *M. Vasalis. Een biografie* [M. Vasalis. A Biography]. Amsterdam: Van
    Oorschot, p. 346.
43 Spanjaard, J. & Mekking, R. (1976). Op. cit., p. 62.

to go underground as well in order to avoid being deported to Germany for "labor deployment." In a 1977 interview in the journal *Vrij Nederland*, Jeanne noted:

> We were actually able to work during the entire war, although in secret. Although my husband was a Jew, according to the race laws we were in a mixed marriage and were "protected" as a result. But we did have to go underground once because we received information that the "Aryan portion" of a mixed marriage had to go "home to the Reich," that is to be part of the labor deployment. But that passed, and we continued to work.[44]

The interviewer then noted that "she is now 81 and still maintains a full schedule with five patients and many supervisions."

International contacts eventually resumed after the liberation, in May 1945. On October 27, 1945 Jeanne was invited by Westerman Holstijn, the secretary of the Dutch Association for Psychiatry and Neurology, to give her first lecture at a training course for psychotherapy titled "The Therapeutic Effect of Psychoanalytic Treatment," which was open to members and junior members only. In December 1945 International Universities Press asked her permission to publish her 1927 paper "The Evolution of the Oedipus Complex in Women" in *The Psychoanalytic Reader*, an anthology of classic articles. Jeanne added a footnote to her article, which was included in her collected works, which were published in 1985 on the occasion of her 90th birthday.[45] This footnote concerned a difference of opinion with Freud regarding his article "Female Sexuality." The Dutch psychoanalyst Hendrika C. Freud wrote a critical and updated version of it.[46]

Jeanne also resumed contact with Marie Bonaparte, whom she had gotten to know well in Vienna. In answer to Jeanne's invitation to give a lecture in Amsterdam, Bonaparte wrote in a letter dated June 23, 1946,

> I heard from Anna [Freud] about your situation during the war. It was much easier for us than for you! During the four years that I lived in the Cape [in South Africa, where she lived from 1941 to 1944], I thought about you often and wondered how you were faring.

44 Pam, M. & Sijmons, R. (1977). "Psychoanalyse. Jeanne Lampl-de Groot heeft nog bij Freud op de divan gelegen" (Psychoanalysis. Jeanne Lampl-de Groot has lain on Freud's Couch). *Vrij Nederland*, 38, 5.

45 Lampl-de Groot, J. (1985). *Man and Mind. Collected Papers of Jeanne Lampl-de Groot.* New York: International Universities Press.

46 Freud, H.C. (1997). *Electra vs Oedipus. The Drama of the Mother-Daughter Relationship.* London: Routledge.

With her international outlook, Jeanne played an important role in reconnecting the associations, which had become isolated as a result of the war. In order to reestablish contact, a European congress was organized in 1947, in Amsterdam, to which French, English, and Swiss psychoanalysts representing various psychoanalytic orientations were invited. The 16th International Congress, the first since 1938, took place in Zurich in 1949. There Jeanne met the German psychoanalyst Alexander Mitscherlich,[47] who invited her to Frankfurt to give a lecture. This contact between Jeanne and Mitscherlich developed into a close long-term collaboration with the Dutch Society and to the reorganization of German psychoanalytic training. It was during this expansive period, in 1958, that Hans Lampl was killed and Jeanne severely injured in an automobile accident. It took months for her to recover sufficiently to be able to resume work.

Regular scientific exchanges with German-speaking colleagues resumed only in the 1960s during the biennial *Arbeitstagung* (workshop) that alternated with the International congresses that since Zurich had rotated among different cities. Other Dutch analysts involved in the workshops included Jaap van der Leeuw, Driek van der Sterren, and Piet Kuiper. All four were involved editorially in the *Jahrbuch für Psychoanalyse*, which resumed publication in 1960. Anna Freud, in her foreword to the first volume, which was aimed at both German-speaking and other analysts, noted that the resumption of publication of the *Jahrbuch* had been the logical consequence of the revival of the psychoanalytic movement in Germany. And while the German Psychoanalytic Association (a branch of the International Association) was celebrating its 10th year, the *Jahrbuch* was celebrating its first.[48] Jeanne Lampl-De Groot's article was on the always relevant topic of depression and aggression, which was undeniably pertinent at the time.[49] Dutch analysts traveled to Germany and gave courses. German colleagues also came to the Netherlands, occasionally staying at Jeanne's summerhouse in Wapenveld. But these activities were not limited only to Germany. Jaap van der Leeuw became president of the International Psychoanalytic Association (IPA) in 1965; Mario Montessori became the secretary. It was a period during which almost all teaching

---

47 Alexander Mitscherlich (1908–1982) played an important role in restoring German psychoanalysis after World War II. In 1947 he and Fred Mielke published *Das Diktat der Menschenverachtung: Eine Dokumentation* (The Dictate of Contempt for Humanity: A Documentation), based on their observation of the Nuremberg Doctors' trial. His most influential work was perhaps *The Inability to Mourn* (1984), which he co-authored with his wife Margarete Mitscherlich-Nielsen. Mitscherlich founded the Sigmund Freud Institut, in Frankfurt, and the German psychoanalytical journal *Psyche*.

48 Freud, A. (1960). *Jahrbuch der Psychoanalyse. Beiträge zur Theorie und Praxis*, vol. I. Cologne: Westdeutscher Verlag, p. VII.

49 Lampl-de Groot, J. (1960). "Depression und Aggression." In K. Draeger, H.E. Richter, G. Scheunert & E. Seeger (eds.), *Jahrbuch der Psychoanalyse. Beiträge zur Theorie und Praxis*, vol. I. Cologne: Westdeutscher Verlag, pp. 145–160.

chairs in psychiatry and child psychiatry at Dutch universities were held by psychoanalysts. Without exception they belonged to a small circle around Jeanne; several of them had undergone training analysis with her. Her international importance was evident from the articles that appeared in a festschrift, written by Heinz Hartmann, Willy Hoffer, Anna Freud, and Alexander Mitscherlich, among others, on the occasion of her 70th birthday.[50]

Over a period of 60 years, Jeanne had produced an almost uninterrupted stream of papers that in sequence provide a fascinating picture of this discipline's historical development. Of course, not all of her works have stood the test of time. During the second feminist wave, some of her older texts sparked controversy. In particular, Jeanne's formulations about the passive, fundamentally masochistic development of women provoked outrage. In fact, this view stood in stark contrast to her own role as an internationally oriented, influential, politically sophisticated, and valiant intellectual woman. The majority of her more than 40 publications were based on interesting clinical observations and insights, which have undoubtedly had an influence on treatment and on psychoanalytic theory. Jeanne proved dynamic enough to correct or revise earlier views. This became especially evident in her revisions regarding the bisexual aspects of Oedipal development, as in her 1982 review article "Thoughts on Psychoanalytic Views of Female Psychology, 1927–1977." Her personal relationships with prominent colleagues, including Heinz Hartmann, Heinz Kohut, Serge Lebovici, and Anna Freud, provided her with a wide-angle view of the scientific landscape, which is reflected in her publications. She always tried to connect understandings from child analysis and infant research with her clinical experience from the analysis of adults, and she was especially fascinated by the ways in which preverbal life experiences presented themselves in adult analysis. Jeanne's attempt to conceptualize the characteristics of the earliest phases of life show a kinship with modern studies on the significance of attachment and mentalization. She liked to engage with the disputes taking place in various theoretical areas of development. The difference between her conception of child development, which derived from her own personal history and insight into child development, and that of Melanie Klein is well known. In Jeanne's eyes Klein's hypotheses were based on an overestimation of the baby's capacities. Although she, like Freud, stressed the importance of the earliest life experiences and object relations – that is, with the mother –, she was unable to agree with the challenging psychiatric concepts that emerged from Kleinian developmental theory, nor with the very earliest

50 Leeuw, P.J. van der, Frijling-Schreuder, E.C.M. & Kuiper, P.C. (eds.). (1967). *Hoofdstukken uit de hedendaagse psychoanalyse* [Chapters in Contemporary Psychoanalysis]. Arnhem: Van Loghum Slaterus.

phases and intensities that played a role in them, and she described them more in terms of Freudian concepts than the Kleinian "paranoid-schizoid position" or "depressive position." Her ideas about the function of guilt feelings in the formation of conscience and their manifestations in adolescence for the psychoanalytic treatment of adults are important and original.

Long after Jeanne had received international acknowledgment – among other things she was made an honorary vice president of the IPA –, she was granted an honorary doctorate by the University of Amsterdam on the occasion of her 75th birthday.

It was not until 1971 that the biennial International Congress took place in Vienna once again. For many psychoanalysts, it was the first time they had set foot in Austria since World War II. A congress took place in Germany for the first time in 1985, in Hamburg. Jeanne's training analysand and professor of child psychiatry at the University of Amsterdam, Bets Frijling-Schreuder, wrote:

> Although she was already frail, she felt obligated to attend the Congress in 1985. The suppression of psychoanalysis under Hitler was sure to be discussed there. And she described how things were back then. Because of the rebuilding work she did during the postwar period, she was made an honorary member of the new German association.[51]

The many international relationships that she had developed, largely with colleagues from her training days in Vienna and Berlin, such as Marianne Kris-Rie, Anna Freud, Dorothy Burlingham, the Hartmanns, with whom she often vacationed, and Margaret Mahler, afforded Jeanne a scientific forum. It is clear that her works came to exhibit interrelationships with those of the people with whom she frequently exchanged ideas, and that she developed particular views, especially regarding child development. She further developed and discussed her ideas as vice president of the IPA and during the many international congresses that she attended. It also became clear to me from the many letters that Jeanne exchanged with Anna Freud during the postwar period up until Anna's death in 1982, that she used her political influence and strategized with Anna.[52] In 1969 Jeanne gave the introductory lecture titled "Thoughts on Advantages and Dangers of 'One-sidedness' in Scientific Research," a plea for the integration of newly acquired insights into Freud's original discoveries. Her text was a condensation of an article published in 1968 in *Psyche* titled

51 Frijling-Schreuder, E.C.M. (1987). "In Memoriam dr. J.A. Lampl-de Groot." *Maandblad Geestelijke volksgezondheid*, 9(87), 971–978.
52 I gained access to copies of these numerous letters in the Edith Berkovits-Lampl Archive.

"Dedicated to Alexander Mitscherlich on the Occasion of His Sixtieth Birthday." It was later included in her *Collected Papers.*[53]

As a result of her efforts, a four-year training program was organized in Amsterdam for child analysts from 1976 to 1980, similar to the one that Anna Freud and the child psychiatrist Jef Teuns had organized in Leiden 10 years earlier with well-known Dutch and English lecturers. In addition to Jeanne, the lecturers included Bets Frijling-Schreuder, David de Levita, and Jet de Levita-Isaac. Moses Laufer, Annemarie and Joseph Sandler, Christopher Dare, and Hansi Kennedy, among others, from the Hampstead Clinic and Tavistock Clinic in London, also gave lectures. Until a year before her death, Jeanne took part in the monthly child analysis working group and participated in its discussions.

Her writings have been anthologized on two separate occasions. The first, *The Development of the Mind*, was published in 1965, when she turned 70, and the second, *Man and Mind*, comprised later works and coincided with her 90th birthday, in 1985. Jeanne gave me a copy of the latter book with the inscription "To Gertie Bögels. With warm thanks to my dear friend. Jeanne Lampl-De Groot." This dedication keeps alive for me many memories of meetings with her. I remember very clearly the first time I saw Jeanne at work: a woman described in a lecture the variants that she saw fit to employ during psychoanalytic treatment. In the following discussion, Jeanne took her to task, explaining in detail why her approach would interfere with the therapeutic efficacy of the analytic setting. In such matters she gave no quarter. An intense discussion followed. Both as a lecturer and supervisor, she enjoyed the back-and-forth of ideas, especially when the other person did not retreat too quickly. Inspired by her aura as someone who had undergone analysis with Freud, I asked her whether she would supervise my first supervised analysis. She had an opening. I remember vividly how impassioned she became when comparing the differences between psychotherapy and psychoanalysis with sessions only once a week and those with four or five sessions a week. There was something of an inspiring master class in the passion with which Jeanne made comments during supervision, stressing in unmistakable terms the importance of the setting to the advancing analytic process, and in her explanation of how "evenly suspended attention" differs from the active intervention by the psychotherapist, an attitude that usually requires the psychiatrist to undergo much training – and finally in the intensity of her mentoring. She had little enthusiasm for combined training in psychoanalysis and psychotherapy, which only later proved to be so fruitful. She feared that as a result too little of what was special about

53 Lampl-de Groot, J. (1985). "Thoughts on Advantages and Dangers of 'One-sidedness' in Scientific Research." In ibid., *Man and Mind. Collected Papers of Jeanne Lampl-de Groot.* New York: International Universities Press, pp. 303–309.

the psychoanalytic setting would be vividly experienced, and that one would fail to recognize its surplus therapeutic value. In 1977, on the occasion of the 60th anniversary of the Dutch Psychoanalytical Society, she gave a lecture in Amsterdam titled "A Birds Eye View of the Past, Present, and Future of Psychoanalysis."[54] She was always pleased to be invited, as when I asked her to give a lecture to the staff of the psychiatric department at the University of Nijmegen, where I was on staff, working as a clinical psychiatrist and psychoanalytic supervisor.

In addition to her original and still inspiring scientific publications, Jeanne Lampl-de Groot's importance for the international psychoanalytic movement consisted in her talent for attracting people to herself and in connecting them with others. Even into old age, she was able to turn professional relationships into personal friendships.

Gertie Bögels, Maarn 2021

Figure 1 Jeanne in her office in the Haringvlietstraat, Amsterdam, October 13, 1942.
(Photo: Frans Dupont, Blaricum [Cousin])

54 This lecture was given on November 24, 1978, in the library of the Kasteel Heyendael Castle, on the grounds of the University of Nijmegen. It is mentioned in her *Collected Papers* (Lampl-de Groot, J. [1985]. Op. cit., p. 425).

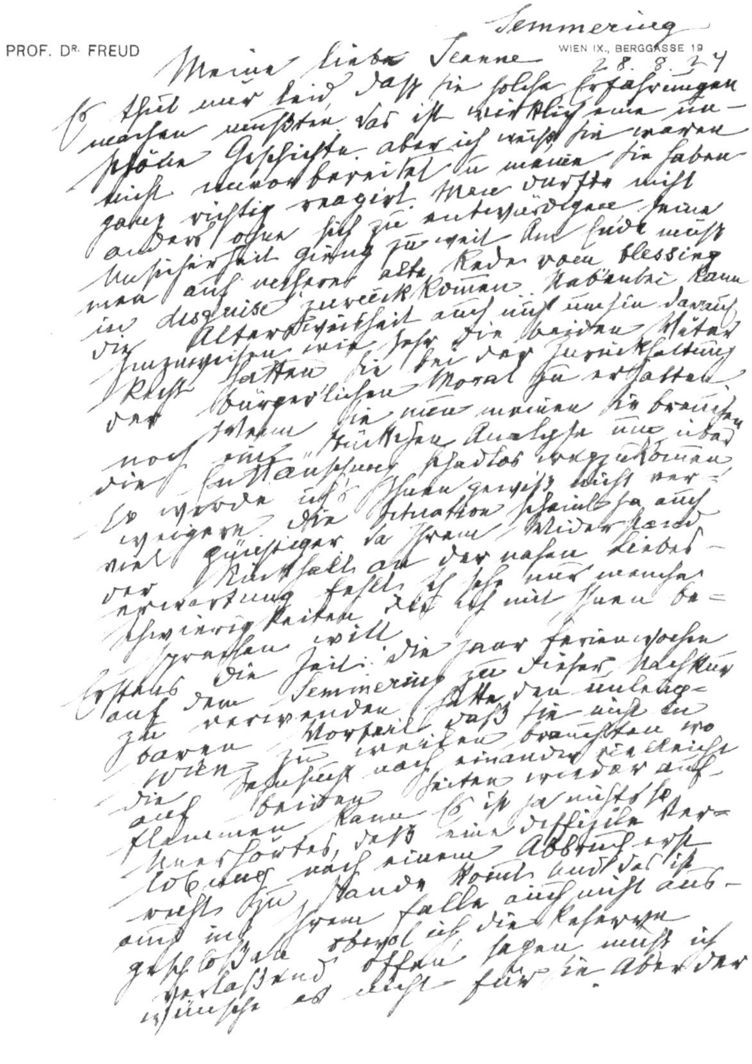

Semmering

PROF. Dr. FREUD

WIEN IX., BERGGASSE 19

28. 8. 24

Meine liebe Jeanne

Figure 2 Letter from Freud, August 28, 1924 (Library of Congress).

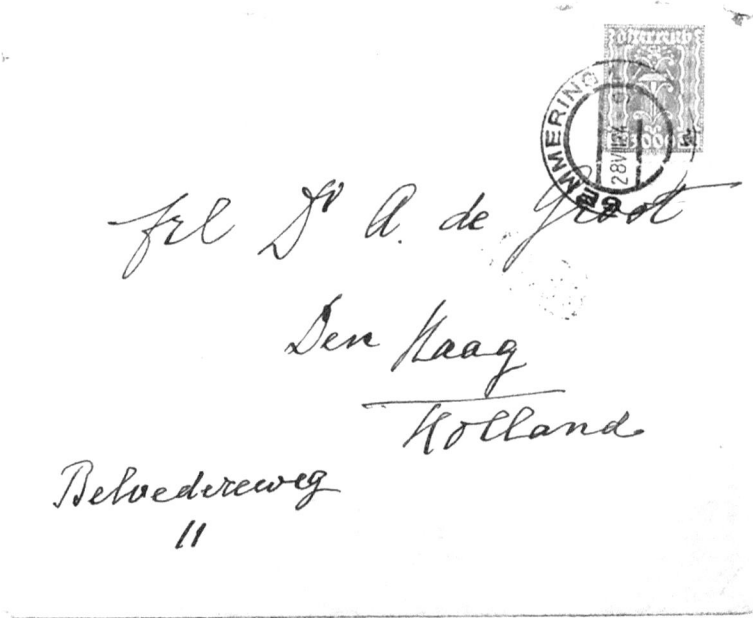

Figure 3 Envelop of letter from Freud to Jeanne de Groot, 1924.

PROF. DR. FREUD
WIEN IX., BERGGASSE 19
*

Figure 4 Freud's return address.

Figure 5 Jeanne with her sisters, 1901 (from left to right: Miek, Henriëtte, Jo, and Jeanne).

Figure 6 Jeanne with her parents, 1933. Henriëtte (right), Edith on her grandmother's lap, cousin Joke behind Henriëtte.

Figure 7 Sigmund Freud in his office, Vienna, 1938.

Figure 8 Jeanne after graduating from medical school, 1921.
Photo: Berssenbrugge, The Hague

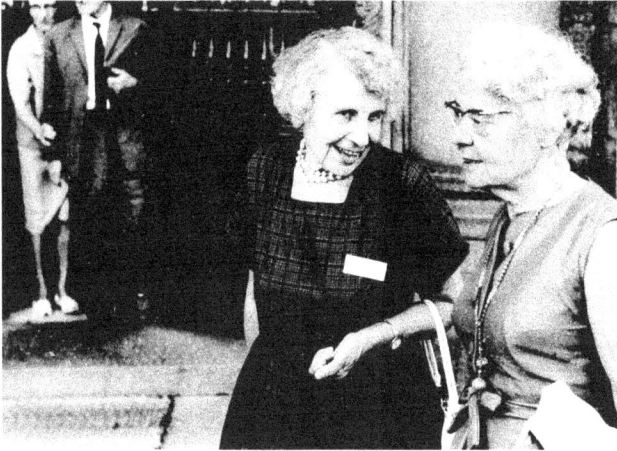

Figure 9 Jeanne with Anna Freud at the IPA Congress, Stockholm, 1963.

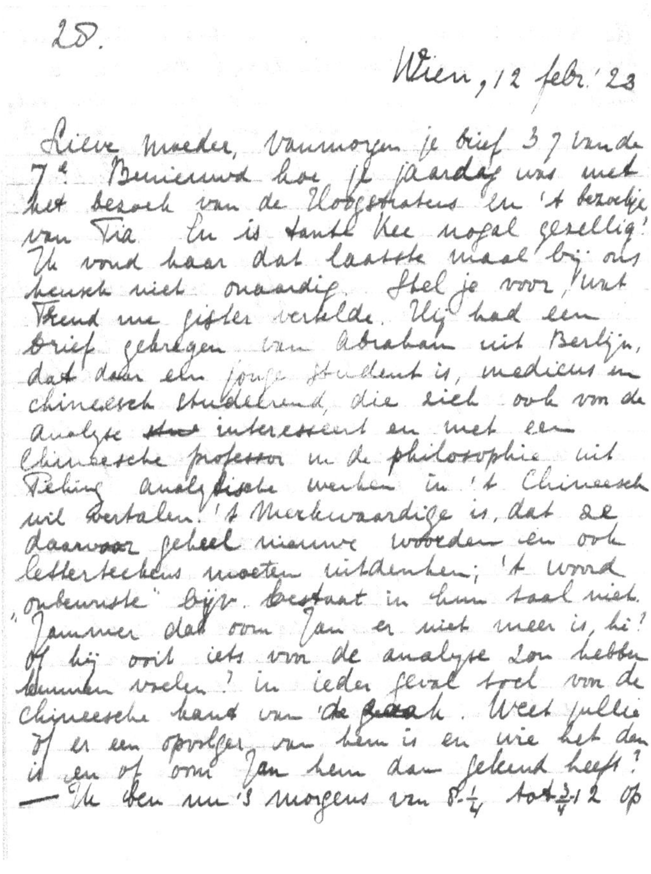

28.

Wien, 12 febr. '23

Lieve moeder, vanmorgen je brief 37 van de
7e. Benieuwd hoe je jaardag was met
het bezoek van de Hoogstratens en 't bezoekje
van Tia. En is tante Kee nogal gezellig?
Ik vond haar dat laatste maal bij ons
heusch niet onaardig. Stel je voor, wat
Freud me gister vertelde. Hij had een
brief gekregen van Abraham uit Berlijn,
dat daar een jonge student is, medicus en
chineesch studeerend, die zich ook voor de
analyse interesseert en met een
Chineesche professor in de philosophie uit
Peking analytische werken in 't Chineesch
wil vertalen. 't Merkwaardige is, dat ze
daarvoor geheel nieuwe woorden en ook
letterteekens moeten uitdenken; 't woord
„onbewuste" bijv. bestaat in hun taal niet.
Jammer dat oom Jan er niet meer is, hè?
Of hij ooit iets van de analyse zou hebben
kunnen voelen? in ieder geval toch van de
Chineesche kant van de zaak. Weet jullie
of er een opvolger van hem is en wie het dan
is en of oom Jan hem dan gekend heeft?
— Ik ben nu 's morgens van 8¼ tot ¾12 op

Figure 10 Letter fragment from Jeanne to her parents, February 12, 1923.

Figure 11 Workshop [*Arbeitstagung*], May 1984. Jaap Wallinga (left), Bien Filet (right).

Figure 12 Jeanne with Han Groen-Prakken (center), the president of the Dutch Psychoanalytic Society.

"My Dear Jeanne"
Sigmund Freud's Letters to Jeanne Lampl-de Groot (1921–1939)

1.
PROF. DR. FREUD, VIENNA IX., BERGGASSE 19.
Seefeld i.T.[1]
September 11, 1921

Dear Doctor,[2]
I always enjoy receiving letters such as yours. At this time I am unable to accept you for analysis because I have no openings, but that fits in well with your intention to spend the next few months in Italy. I would probably be able to find time for you between January and Easter, and I will write to your home address to ask whether you can come. At issue is a considerable piece of preparatory work for psychoanalysis, that is, self-analysis. While doing that, you may read the literature, attend lectures, and take part in meetings.

After the end of your autoanalysis it is recommended that you go to Berlin to become familiarized with the treatment of ill patients at the psychoanalytical polyclinic there. You may also do all of your training in Berlin, for which everything has been prepared.[3]

---

1 Seefeld, a village in Tyrol, was a holiday resort favored by the Freuds.
2 Freud's first letter to Jeanne shows, among other things, how easy it was back then for candidates to apply for training. His letter was addressed to "Frl. Dr. Jeanne de Groot, Belvédèreweg 11, Den Haag," her parents' home. Freud's answer is courteous and at the same time personal and matter-of-fact. It also shows that even then training analysis (Freud calls it "autoanalysis" here) was viewed as a mandatory part of the training. The German address "Fräulein Doktor" (lit. Miss Doctor) will be dispensed with in the translation.
3 The Berlin Polyclinic along with the Training Institute and library opened more than a year earlier, on February 14, 1920, thanks to the generosity of Max Eitingon. Freud's son Ernst was the architect; he performed the necessary renovations. According to Jones, Freud did not consider Vienna a suitable center for psychoanalysis; that, however, did not prevent a clinic (called the Ambulatorium) from opening there two years later, on May 22, 1922 (Jones, E. [1957]. *The Life and Work of Sigmund Freud*, vol. 3. New York: Basic Books, pp. 20–21).

DOI: 10.4324/9781003268130-3

With best wishes for the realization of your plans
Your devoted
Freud

[Addressed to:]
Frl. Dr. Jeanne de Groot
Belvedereweg 11, The Hague, Holland

1a
Between these first two letters there is a sheet of paper on which Lampl-de Groot wrote:
"All of my letters to Freud were destroyed in the spring of 1938 after the annexation [of Austria] to Hitler. JL.deGr."

2.
PROF. DR. FREUD, VIENNA IX., BERGGASSE 19.
Christmas 1921

Dear Doctor,[4]
Your worries are baseless, and your wishes are in part congruent with mine.

Vienna is calm, and foreigners have as little to fear here as, for example, in an Italian city. The riots occurred on one afternoon and haven't been repeated. To the extent that we may predict the future, this worry should be allayed.

Unfortunately, lodgings are not easy to find here, although all of my foreigners have eventually found a place. Prolongation of your stay in Italy works very well for me. I would not yet have an opening at the end of January, and you are third in line on my list. As a result, Easter works well. We must therefore ensure that the beginning of your analysis not be postponed for too long. I will interrupt my work from July 14 (perhaps even July 1) to October 1, and 2–3 months is too little time for you in any case. You would have to return in the fall. If you wished to spend more time, I can provide you with excellent didactic analysis[5] with one of my female students here. Please write to me of your intentions.

With best wishes, and some envy, for your stay in Italy,
Your devoted Freud

---

4 The second letter is dated "Christmas 1921." Apparently, Jeanne was worried about safety in Vienna, which is also evident from her letter to her mother from Rome on December 13, 1921. Freud tried to reassure her – ironically by pointing to the same insecurities prevalent in Italian cities at the time.

5 This was Freud's term for "training analysis" at the time.

[Addressed to:]
Frl. Dr. Jeanne de Groot
Pension Primrose, 6 Via Montebello, Rome
Please forward!
[Forwarded to:] Pension du Midi Piazza Amedeo, Naples

3.
PROF. DR. FREUD, VIENNA IX., BERGGASSE 19.
December 24, 1923

Dear Doctor,[6]
I am permitted to work again, and I invite you to visit me on Monday, December 31 between 3 and 3:30 to schedule the session. Our analysis may then be continued on January 2.

In the hope that your waiting time has not become too boring, I send you warm greetings.

Your Freud

[Addressed to:]
Frl. Dr. Jeanne de Groot, p.A. Frau Hofrat Frisch
Vienna VIII., Josefstadterstrasse 17

6 This letter is dated exactly two years after the previous one: in 1923, one day before Christmas, after analysis had been underway for a while, which, however, had had to be interrupted because of Freud's illness. In February 1923 Freud had self-diagnosed cancer in his right upper jaw and right gum. Surgery was performed in April 1923, followed by a larger operation in October. This was the first of numerous more or less complex treatments, excisions, x-rays, and radium treatments. Removal of the cancerous tissue, the excruciating pain, the anesthetizing drugs, and later the fitted gum prosthesis were to become an ongoing torture. The association between smoking and cancer had already been recognized at the time. Shortly after the first surgery, Freud decided to visit Rome in September together with his daughter Anna, a trip that he had long wished to undertake. The risks to his health, of which both were aware, were very real. During one breakfast, "Suddenly a stream of blood spurted from Freud's mouth, a hard crust having evidently loosened a piece of tissue." Nonetheless, Freud wrote, "Rome was very lovely, especially the first two weeks before the sirocco came and increased my pain." (Jones, E. [1957]. Op. cit., vol. 3, p. 94).

The salutation and the concluding greeting are significantly more personal; the "Fräulein" has changed to "Frau Doktor," and the conclusion from "Ihr ergebener Freud" (Your devoted Freud) to the more familiar "Ihr Freud" (Your Freud). A year later until the end of their correspondence, the letters are identical in terms of openness and cordiality, with only minor variations on "herzlich, Ihr Freud" (Warmly, Your Freud) – with one exception, a postcard dated March 15, 1933, which concludes, perhaps jokingly, "alte, taube xx" (old deaf xx).

4.
PROF. DR. FREUD, VIENNA IX., BERGGASSE 19.
Semmering[7]
August 28, 1924

My dear Jeanne,

I am sorry that you have had to endure such experiences. That really is an unpleasant story. But I know that you weren't unprepared, and I think that you responded quite correctly. One could not do otherwise without disgracing oneself; his insecurity went too far. In the end we have to fall back on our old saying about blessings in disguise. Besides, the wisdom of old age cannot help but point out how right the two fathers were in advising you to maintain the reserve of bourgeois morality.[8]

If you now think that you need another "little bit" of analysis in order to get over your disappointment without harm, I would certainly not deny it to you. The situation seems much more favorable, because your resistance lacks the reinforcement of a close expectation of love. I see only a few difficulties, which I will discuss with you.

First, the time: to use the few weeks of vacation in Semmering for this follow-up treatment would have the undeniable advantage that you wouldn't have to stay in Vienna, where the yearning for each other, possibly mutual, might flare up again. It is not that uncommon for a difficult engagement to come about after a breakup. And in your case [!] that is not out of the question either, although, leaving my reserve behind, I must say that I do not wish it upon you. Unfortunately, however, September is not available for your treatment. Prof. Pichler[9] will be returning in midmonth, and then I must be prepared to spend every second or third day in Vienna because the prosthesis no longer fits and it requires adjustments; renewed radiation treatment is also envisioned. (My sense of well-being has certainly improved greatly.) I have also given time off from September 15 to October 1 to the one patient whom I brought here with me. October is all that remains in Vienna. Then there is the second question, that of money. For the fall I have accepted four persons at $20, but I am prepared to postpone or give up one of them for you. However then it is only right to ask that you pay the same fee that the session would otherwise have brought me. The increase would certainly have an abbreviating effect and prevent you from spending the time in fruitless yearning for abandoned expectations. That you will be in the same place as him and might meet again is an unpleasant circumstance with which one must come to terms.

---

7 Semmering is a ski and health resort about 60 miles southwest of Vienna, where Freud was recovering from a respiratory infection after a bout of the grippe.
8 Freud appears to want to protect her from the indecisiveness of her suitors.
9 Hans Pichler (1877–1949), ear, nose, and throat specialist who operated on Freud numerous times. His treatment records are extant (see Jones, E. [1957]. Op. cit., vol. 3, pp. 468–495).

Think about it and let me know soon what you have decided.

Please convey my regards to your parents, and with warm wishes for your well-being, Sincerely your Freud.

[Addressed to:]
Frl. Dr. A. de Groot, The Hague, Holland, Belvedereweg 11

5.
PROF. DR. FREUD, VIENNA IX., BERGGASSE 19
Semmering
September 6, 1924

My dear Jeanne,
Thank you for acknowledging my concerns, which necessitate postponing until October.

But now to the new situation! You are correct that it changes much. Although I was prepared that this might happen – you recall the passage in my letter –, but I hadn't expected it so soon, not before we had completed our follow-up work. You ask my opinion regarding how you should behave. That's not easy to say. I would have lost the desire long ago, and my trust would have disappeared given these continuous vacillations, but I cannot feel my way into the soul of a girl who is in love to the extent that I could hit upon the right thing to do. What seems certain to me is that responsiveness on your part – especially in the geographic sense – would be a terrible mistake and rob you of the last shred of independence. In addition, the suspicion with which you receive the suggestion of a rendezvous in Florence seems well-founded.

But now, as you correctly recognize, the new situation brings with it the risk that the intended follow-up treatment would proceed exactly the same as the earlier work, with the reinforcement of the young man's resistance, and become completely dependent on his vacillations or his insistencies, and be prolonged for some undetermined time. I don't want to have that happen again, but I see only one way to avoid it, a path that will be difficult for you, and that for me will create great initial resistance in you.[10] But there is nothing else to be done. I think you will understand what I mean. All interactions with him must *cease* completely, not only during this vacation, but also afterwards for the

---

10 Freud is apparently saying that her hesitation may possibly be "neurotically conditioned," and that this would have to be worked through before she would be capable of an unambiguous choice. Neurotic hesitation supposedly increases resistance to psychoanalysis, it being a kind of alibi, a not-having-to-know that it is her own hesitation. Freud's views on this and his extensive efforts to establish personal relationships during psychoanalysis would be unthinkable today and are viewed as unacceptable.

duration of treatment. In other words, either you come to an agreement with him beforehand, in which case you hardly need the treatment – or his punishment must be prolonged a bit longer, that is, it consists in his disappearing from the scene as long as you are engaged in analysis. With this condition I am merely creating the setting that each analysis requires and which I had foregone in favor of the possibility of your happiness.

I hope that you will have understood me this time as well.

Sincerely, your Freud.

[Addressed to:]
Frl. Dr. A. de Groot, The Hague, Holland, Belvedereweg 11

6.
PROF. DR. FREUD, VIENNA IX., BERGGASSE 19
February 16, 1925

Dear Jeanne,

I heard today that you are staying at home for another week. Time to send you a few lines meant to provide you with my best wishes for your next stage – Berlin.

Eitingon[11] visited me, and I had the opportunity to speak to him about you. One of my sons, Ernst, lives in Berlin with his very nice wife and their three sons named after the archangels (Regentenstr. 23).[12] I hope that you will find your way there. You will probably not engage in superfluous correspondence with Vienna, as with Jan I? I would advise against it.

With warm greetings in the expectation of hearing from you.

Your Freud.

[Addressed to:]
Frl. Dr. A. de Groot, The Hague, Holland, Belvedereweg 11
[Forwarded:] Hotel Hessler, Kantstrasse 166, Berlin 10

11 Max Eitingon (1881–1943) lived in Berlin from 1909 to 1933. He did his psychiatric and psychoanalytic training at the Burghölzli Clinic in Zurich, among other places. He was wealthy, a confidant of Freud, and a prominent member and later president of the IPA. In addition, he sponsored the Berlin Psychoanalytical Polyclinic, which was founded in 1920.
12 Ernst Freud (1892–1970), his wife Lucie (Lux) Brasch (1896–1989), and three sons, Stephen Gabriel, (1921–2015), Lucian Michael (1922–2011), who later became a painter, and Clemens Raphael (1924–2009).

7.
PROF. DR. FREUD, VIENNA IX., BERGGASSE 19
March 3, 1925

Dear Jeanne,

I am including the special offprint of The "Autobiography"[13] that you asked for, primarily because you were so good and sensible as not to correspond with Jan II (or III). Don't show this little book to anyone in Berlin because, except for you, the only people who have received it there are Abraham,[14] Eitingon, and Sachs,[15] and it is the only copy that I have other than my own.

I hope that by now you have become the complete Berliner. It made me happy that you visited Ernst. You have gotten to know two young men there whom I do not yet know.

With warm wishes
Your Freud

[Addressed to:]
Herr Dr. H. Lampl[16]
for Frl. Dr. J. de Groot, Berlin, Blumeshof 16

13 Freud, S. (1925). "An Autobiographical Study." In *Standard Edition*, vol. XX. London: Hogarth, pp. 7–74. Here Freud endeavors "to construct a narrative in which subjective and objective attitudes, biographical and historical interests, are combined in a new proportion." (Ibid., p. 7). It is a biography that is simultaneously an incisive description of his scientific development and of the development of psychoanalysis as a science. In his "Postscript" (1935) to the "Autobiographical Study," Freud writes in this connection, "Shortly before I wrote this study it seemed as though my life would soon be brought to an end by the recurrence of a malignant disease; but surgical art saved me in 1923 and I was able to continue my life and my work, though no longer in freedom from pain." (Freud, S. [1925]. "Postscript" to the "Autobiographical Study." In op. cit., pp. 71–74).
14 Karl Abraham (1877–1925), a psychoanalyst highly respected by Freud, received his psychiatric training at the Burghölzli Clinic, in Zurich. With Max Eitingon, he was cofounder of the first psychoanalytical polyclinic in Berlin, of which he later became director, and he was founder and, until his premature death, president of the Berlin Psychoanalytical Association, and president of the International Psychoanalytical Association (1920). (Bentick van Schoonheten, A. [2016]. *Karl Abraham: Life and Work, a Biography*. London: Karnac, pp. xxiii, 432).
15 Hanns Sachs (1881–1947), a Viennese lawyer, was from 1910 on a member of the Viennese Psychoanalytical Association. He represented Otto Rank during the latter's military service as primary publisher of the *Internationale Zeitschrift für Psychoanalyse*. Starting in 1920 Sachs worked as a psychoanalyst and was the first training analyst in Berlin. He was Hans Lampl's analyst. In 1932 he emigrated to Boston, and he died in 1947 at the age of 66 from the effects of chronic tuberculosis.
16 Hans Lampl (1889–1958) studied medicine, and for eight years worked together with the hematologist Dr. Landsteiner, before starting his psychoanalytic training in Berlin. He was a fellow student and friend of Freud's son Martin, and for years was treated as a member of the Freud family. In an interview with Lampl conducted by Kurt Eissler in the early 1950s, he noted that "I was friends with all six children . . .. They treated me

8.
PROF. DR. FREUD, VIENNA IX., BERGGASSE 19
May 10, 1925

My dear ones!
A birthday letter, even when written on a new machine, is not nearly as strenuous as a birthday itself. With writing one becomes ever more practiced with time; hopefully this is also the case with life itself.

Without any warning, an unbelievable magnificence of roses arrived under the name Jeanne, for which I thank you. I wish you both the continuation of all that is good!

Warmly, Freud.

[Addressed to:]
Herr and Frau Dr. Lampl
Berlin W.10, Friedrich Wilhelmstrasse 4
Pension Krause

9.
PROF. DR. FREUD, VIENNA IX., BERGGASSE 19
June 19, 1925

My dear Jeanne,
Delighted! I may say that we all are about the good news. It is wonderful that this wish of yours has been fulfilled so soon; you had a right to it in every respect. And you yourself know that there is no reason to fear a disturbance.

---

more or less like a child in the house. I was actually there almost the entire day, when I wasn't in school" (Edith Berkovits-Lampl Archive). He participated in holiday excursions, and on these occasions, Freud taught him to identify mushrooms, something that Freud reminded him of in this correspondence. Eitingon, Freud, and his daughter Anna respected him as a physician. See Freud, S. & Eitingon, M. (2004). *Briefwechsel 1906–1939*. Ed. Michael Schröter. Tübingen: edition diskord, pp. 269–270. It is known that he unsuccessfully sought the hand of Freud's daughter Sophie. Later he fell in love with Anna. But after various girlfriends, as Freud described Anna's lesbianism with some ambivalence in a letter to Eitingon on November 11, 1921, Anna developed "an understandable thirst for female friendship, but I wish that she would soon find reason to trade her attachment to her old father for something more permanent" (ibid., p. 267). Eissler's interview contains charming domestic descriptions of the Freud family's daily life. The Dutch psychoanalyst Mario Montessori wrote an "In Memoriam" after Lampl's death in which he described Lampl's development and cited his many contributions to the psychoanalytic organization (Montessori, M.M. [1960]. "Dr. Hans Lampl 1889–1958." *International Journal of Psychoanalysis*, 41, 163–164).

You need not make a narcissistic annoyance[17] out of the signs of inner resistance against this new state – which after all has already diminished. It is certainly something that is unconscious, but probably so deep-rooted that one cannot grasp it, something that one might almost call organic because it represents an inherited resistance, not an individually acquired or strengthened one. It may be the last offshoot of dissatisfaction from the Oedipus complex. We know too little about it.

Naturally, the two of you will be happy and silly parents, and hopefully you will have reason to be. The question of destiny, what [the child] will become, will be decided today, long before it becomes manifest.

I know that you are having a house built in Grunewald.[18] When will it be finished? It's too bad that I no longer think of traveling.

So I really won't be traveling to Homburg,[19] but Anna will be there. My tortures promise to remit; however, enough remain to justify the need for caution. Basically, I ask little more than not to be reminded of it constantly.

Please give my greetings to big Hans, and accept my warmest wishes for your further well-being, from your Freud.

[Addressed to:]
Frau Dr. Jeanne Lampl-de Groot
Berlin W.10, Friedrich Wilhelmstrasse 4
Pension Krause

10.
Semmering, Südbahnhotel mit Blick auf Rax, 2009 m. u. Schneeberg, 2075 m.
Semmering
July 20, 1925

Many thanks for your warm letters and today's floral greeting. We feel very comfortable here.
Your Freud.

[Addressed to:]
Herr and Frau Dr. Lampl
Selvagardena (Wolkenstein), Hotel Oswald, Italy

---

17 Signs of pregnancy are meant here.
18 A wooded neighborhood in Berlin-Charlottenburg.
19 Bad Homburg, where the 9th International Psychoanalytical Congress took place from September 2–5. This is where Anna Freud read her father's "Psychological Consequences of the Anatomical Distinction between the Sexes," and Eitingon formulated the international methods and standards for candidates for psychoanalytic training (Jones, E. [1957]. Op. cit., p. 112).

11.
[Picture postcard with text:]
Semmering
August 3, 1925

Rampion[20] arrived fresh, edelweiss and artemisia very beautiful. Envy and warm thanks.
Your Freud.

[Addressed to:]
Herr, Frau Dr. H. Lampl de Groot
Selva Val Gardena (Wolkenstein), Hotel Oswald, Italy

12.
PROF. DR. FREUD, VIENNA IX., BERGGASSE 19
December 28, 1925

My dear Jeanne,
First of all, my children's visit brought me first-hand news that you are well and that you are not showing, something that women are so proud of!
A Dutch woman who calls herself "Jeanne's mother" sent me by circuitous path a box of those good cigars that are still produced in Holland. When you write to the lady again, please don't forget to convey my warmest thanks for this Christmas gift.
Our pleasure in these days was naturally disturbed by the unhappy outcome of Abraham's illness.[21] If I were capable of traveling I would have seen you again in your new setting.
With warm wishes for you and your big Hans for the significant year 1926.
Your Freud

[Addressed to:]
Frau Dr. A. Lampl-de Groot
Berlin, Hohenzollernstr. 14

20 Rampion and artemisia are medicinal plants.
21 Karl Abraham died on December 25, 1925.

13.
PROF. DR. FREUD, VIENNA IX., BERGGASSE 19
February 11, 1926

My dear ones!
Although it was to be predicted that Jeanne would pass her great test flawlessly[22] and excellently fulfill the duties arising from it, we are natural scientists and confirmation by experience must remain more meaningful than the assured expectation. Of course, I was very happy to hear that everything is going so well, and I even think that given the status of the sexes today it makes no difference whether the baby is manifestly male or female. Especially because a significant preponderance in one direction may be compensated for, as desired, by the results of subsequent experiments.
My warmest greetings to all three members of the happy association!
Your Freud

[Addressed to:]
Herr and Frau
Dr. H. J. Lampl, <u>Berlin</u> W.10, Hohenzollernstr. 14

14.
PROF. DR. FREUD, VIENNA IX., BERGGASSE 19
June 3, 1926

I don't believe I have written you at your new address yet. I like to think of you as a housewife; I've already seen you as a little mother, and I am glad that Ernst[23] has largely arranged things to your liking.
I correctly understood your silence as an attempt to protect me, which is something I needed, because we just finished with our obligatory responses on May 31.[24] But if I missed something, I have been richly

---

22 I.e., the birth of Henriëtte, also called Harriet, on January 30, 1926.
23 Freud's son Ernst (1892–1970) was an architect and lived in Berlin from 1920 to 1932. He emigrated to London in 1933. Ernst designed and built the "Villa Lampl" especially for Jeanne and Hans, with two practice rooms. The house is still standing, now with a renovated roof (originally a flat roof, now with a peaked gable). Although the name of the street was changed to Waldmeisterstraße, the house number has remained the same. The roof was damaged during World War II and restored in a changed form. Unfortunately, the new owners have refused permission for a memorial plaque (as per a 2011 e-mail from Regine Lockot, Berlin).
24 I.e., responses to birthday greetings.

compensated by letters and pictures. The new photograph succeeded in expressing your inner happiness. Who was the artist?

We will be going up to the Villa Schüler in Semmering on the 16th or 17th of this month. I would be feeling quite well except for the stupid, technical tortures of the prosthesis. It seems that I have gotten over my recent cardiac symptoms. Nonetheless, this remains a nice opportunity.

With satisfaction we heard about the positive outcome of your good mother-in-law's surgery.

Please convey my greetings to big Hans; little Harriet probably doesn't place much value on a greeting yet, as she is still one with her sole object.[25] Think of me and write again soon,

With warm regards,

Freud

[Addressed to:]
Frau Dr. Jeanne Lampl-de Groot
Berlin-Dahlem, Strasse 88b beim Roseneck

15.
PROF. DR. FREUD, VIENNA IX., BERGGASSE 19
July 25, 1926

My dear Jeanne,

I think I should answer you before the pre-announced pictures of the children arrive. We don't often experience such a lovely, free Sunday morning.

I enjoy hearing your descriptions of your youthful happiness. It is clear that your little daughter now gives you more material than your big man. In his astute frivolity, Rank[26] would surely ascribe both anxiety attacks to the baby's fears during childbirth, triggered by immersion in warm bathwater. But he wouldn't be able to explain why this reaction occurred at two random times and not during the first times that she was bathed. They were probably the result of pain from intestinal spasms that began in the bath. Pain and fear are often not easily distinguishable in infants. There is

---

25 The theory at the time was that the mother was the primary object.

26 Otto Rank (1884–1939), né Rosenfeld, was secretary of the Vienna Psychoanalytical Association from 1906 to 1915. He and Sándor Ferenczi published the *Internationale Zeitschrift für Psychoanalyse* from its founding in 1913, and from 1921 to 1924 he was the sole publisher. The journal ceased publication in 1941. During his military service, he was represented by Hanns Sachs; Rank served as editor of the *Krakauer Zeitung*, the official organ of the Austrian army. After the publication of his very controversial *The Trauma of Birth* (1923) Rank broke with classical psychoanalysis. Sándor Radó (1890–1972) took over the editorship; Rank emigrated to the United States in 1934.

no need for us to rack our brains about her future upbringing. Where love and understanding coexist, the necessary middle path between tolerance and discouragement will be easy to find. Sparing the necessary repressions cannot be at issue here.

It is very pleasant here to the extent that the changeable weather allows. The villa next to ours is occupied by the mother of Anna's American children,[27] who brought a Ford with her, and because the reserve that otherwise exists between patient and analyst is not possible with children, we have a very pleasant neighborly relationship. During the first three weeks of our stay I wrote a pamphlet on the question of lay analysis, provoked by the accusation of quackery against Dr. Reik,[28] which provided our newspapers with a lot of fodder. My French-Greek princess (Marie Bonaparte)[29] has been here for the past 14 days; she appears called to have a great influence on the development of analysis in France. I am feeling good, but too often bothered by swelling at the scars. The other family members after whom you ask are doing very well too. Wolf[30] is very tame and lovable, but surely regrets the muzzle, which he is forced to wear because of the danger of rabies. Even our most distant visitors are aware of his heroic deed, how, after he had gotten lost in Vienna he jumped into an automobile and insisted on being driven home. He had no money on him, but his address was on the collar around his neck.

27 Dorothy Tiffany Burlingham (1891–1979). Her daughters were in psychoanalytic treatment with Anna Freud. Dorothy Burlingham became Anna's life partner (Young-Bruehl, E. [1988]. *Anna Freud: A Biography*. New York: Summit Books, pp. 132–133).
28 Theodor Reik (1888–1969) studied psychology, literature, philosophy, and theology, and was in training analysis with Karl Abraham. He was a (lay) training analyst at the psychoanalytical institutes in Vienna and Berlin. He fled Nazi persecution in 1934, first to Holland, and then in 1938 to New York. The term *lay analyst* indicates that he was not a licensed physician. As a result of a suit brought against Reik for "quackery" – based on an old Austrian law whereby treating patients without being licensed as a physician was forbidden – Freud wrote a fiery rebuttal in defense of lay analysis. In it he noted the general lack of knowledge of physicians with regard to the psychological and psychodynamic aspects of medicine, and he stressed the intensive training that analysts must go through in order to become training analysts. See Freud, S. (1926). "The Question of Lay Analysis: Conversations with an Impartial Person." In *Standard Edition*, vol. XX. London: Hogarth, pp. 183–250.
29 Marie Bonaparte (1882–1962) was well known, and by way of her maternal grandfather Francois Blanc, came to own the Casino in Monte Carlo, as a result of which she became very wealthy. Her great-grandfather was one of Napoleon's brothers. Married to George, Prince of Greece, she was an extravagant woman who became a politically influential psychoanalyst. She became a friend of the Freud family and played an important role in facilitating Freud's forced flight to England. She also interceded with then Dutch princess Juliana on behalf of the Lampl-de Groots. (Stouten, H. [2011]. *Marie Bonaparte 1882–1962. Freuds prinses zoekt haar dode moeder* [Freud's Princess Looks for Her Dead Mother]. Amsterdam: Amsterdam University Press, p. 172). Her name is in parentheses in the original letter.
30 A German shepherd.

Greetings to you, Hans, and Harriet
Warmly, your Freud.

[Addressed to:]
Frau Dr. Jeanne Lampl-de Groot
Braunwald Haus Tanneggli
Kanton Glarus, Schweiz

16.
PROF. DR. FREUD, VIENNA IX., BERGGASSE 19
February 22, 1927

My dear Jeanne,
Don't be surprised at my belated response to your lovely "birthday letter." I'm going through a fallow period right now when absolutely nothing I do pleases me. This is almost certainly because the new prosthesis
isn't finished yet, and the old one is a horrific torture.

Your daughter is a little beauty, and I especially liked her earnest expression. A beauty need not be laughing, although mothers like to see them
that way. What is it about these little creatures that makes them so charming? After all, we have experienced all sorts of things from them that don't
comport with our ideals, and must see them as little animals. But of course,
animals seem charming to us and much more attractive than complicated,
multistory adult humans. I'm experiencing that right now with our Wolf,
who almost replaces our deceased Heinele.[31]

In Berlin, I found that little Eva[32] might turn into something similar.

Anna's book will be published soon,[33] and she herself will be able to
visit your home and child. My trip to Berlin was full of pleasant experiences and resulted in no afterpains. My visit with you was so completely
satisfying that I can only wish that it always remain so lovely.

Greetings to you, Hans, and Harriet, sincerely
Your Freud

[Addressed to:]
Frau Dr. Jeanne Lampl-de Groot
Berlin-Dahlem, Strasse 88b beim Roseneck

31 Heinz Rudolf (dim. Heinele), the son of Max Halberstadt and Freud's favorite daughter,
Sophie, died of acute miliary tuberculosis in June 1923.
32 Eva (1924–1944) was the daughter of Freud's son Oliver (1891–1969) and Henny Fuchs.
33 Freud, A. (1928). *Introduction to the Technique of Child Analysis.* New York: Ayer.

17.
PROF. DR. FREUD, VIENNA IX., BERGGASSE 19
March 3, 1927

My dear Jeanne,
I was very pleased with your first intellectual offspring. It turned out well. I hope that others will follow it. And on that note, I really don't know whether you are right concerning your revision of my claim. It could easily be; sounds very plausible. At least in a number of cases, those that demonstrate a stronger tendency toward virility. But perhaps really generally, but we need a lot more observation to draw conclusions. In any case, your interpretation and description are very justified.[34]

There is one point in which you could still improve the text, by sharply stressing the contrast to my previous paper, in the process adding other congruences. There are a few small inconsistencies in your German style, which your husband could correct in order to spare Radó[35] the work. – I don't place much value on your argument that the boy saves himself for later by foregoing the possibility in the present; it seems much too clever, and unlikely given his age.[36]

34 Freud is referring to Jeanne Lampl's paper "The Evolution of the Oedipus Complex in Women" (1927/1928). *International Journal of Psychoanalysis*, 9, 332–345, which lays out Lampl's revision of Freud's theory of penis envy. Lampl pointed out that girls have comparable sexual feelings and experiences, and that, analogous to boys and their penis, they are activated by the clitoris and vagina. Lampl considered girls' relationships to their mothers to be more "complex" and "intense" than did Freud. In her paper she also referred to the findings of another analyst, Karen Horney, who pointed out that the fact that males had up to then been the ones making the analytical observations also played a role. In addition, in *Electra vs Oedipus: The Drama of the Mother-Daughter Relationship* (2011), the Dutch psychoanalyst Hendrika C. Freud described the mother-daughter relationship as "more complex" than either Lampl-de Groot or Sigmund Freud. In his 1931 paper "Female Sexuality," Sigmund Freud wrote, "It does indeed appear that women analysts – as, for instance, Jeanne Lampl-de Groot and Helene Deutsch – have been able to perceive these facts more easily and clearly because they are helped in dealing with those under their treatment by the transference to a suitable mother-substitute. Nor have I succeeded in seeing my way through any case completely, and I shall therefore confine myself to reporting the most general findings and shall give only a few examples of the new ideas which I have arrived at. . . . . I am in agreement with the principal points in Jeanne Lampl-de Groot's (1927) important paper. In this the complete identity of the pre-Oedipus phase in boys and girls is recognized, and the girl's sexual (phallic) activity towards her mother is affirmed and substantiated by observations." See Freud, S. [1931]. "Female Sexuality." In *Standard Edition*, vol. XXI. London: Hogarth, pp. 226–227, 241).
35 Sándor Radó (1890–1972) was a Hungarian psychoanalyst, secretary of the Hungarian branch of the IPA from its founding in 1913; after 1924 he was editor of the *Internationale Zeitschrift für Psychoanalyse*.
36 I.e., giving up Oedipal desires.

What is going to happen with your manuscript? Should I send it to you or to the editors?

Warm greetings to your triad![37]

Freud

[Addressed to:]
Frau Dr. Jeanne Lampl-de Groot
Berlin-Dahlem, Schumacherplatz (Strasse 88b b. Roseneck)

18.
PROF. DR. FREUD, VIENNA IX., BERGGASSE 19
June 11, 1927

My dear Jeanne,

I can't write as often as Harriet is photographed, but I gladly confirm that she presents herself as a magnificent girl (in all company), and I am always glad – not only – each time that she introduces herself! My wife is collecting all of the pictures.

I know Gargellen[38] from a research trip many years ago. It is very high. We will be going to Semmering on the 16th.

Warm greetings to the three of you, from your
Freud

[Addressed to:]
Frau Dr. Jeanne Lampl-de Groot
Berlin-Dahlem, Strasse 88b beim Roseneck

19.
PROF. DR. FREUD, VIENNA IX., BERGGASSE 19
November 2, 1927

My dear Jeanne,

Your letter tells me nothing that we hadn't been prepared for. Nonetheless, it remains a happy message, and the wishes that it elicits can only be, may the new not fall short of the previous, whether or not it exceeds the

---

37 In *Introductory Lectures on Psycho-Analysis*, the word *triad* is used in describing a detailed dream in which a house is broken into: "You will have no trouble in recognizing the symbols used. The male genitals are represented by a triad of figures, and the female ones by a landscape with a chapel, hill and wood. Once again you will find steps as the symbol for the sexual act. What is called a hill in the dream is also called one in anatomy – the Mons Veneris [the Hill of Venus]." See Freud, S. (1916). "Introductory Lectures on Psycho-Analysis." In *Standard Edition*, vol. XV. London: Hogarth, p. 193).

38 Gargellen is an Alpine village in Vorarlberg, Austria.

latter in terms of sex. You will notice that I do not claim to be a feminist. It will certainly be a painful experience for Harriet, but whoever loves her should not wish that she be spared that. It belongs to life, and in the end she will gain much from it.

Given your wonderful health, you will have an easy time until the arrival of the new one.

With many warm greetings for all of you, but this time for you in particular, Your Freud

[Addressed to:]
Frau Dr. Jeanne Lampl-de Groot
Berlin-Dahlem, Schumacherplatz 2

20.
PROF. DR. FREUD, VIENNA IX., BERGGASSE 19
June 2, 1929

Dear Jeanne,
I have to admit that I was very surprised when I first saw the picture enclosed with your letter. Did you really, with unlimited ambition, permit yourself a third child because the first two had turned out so well?[39] That didn't make sense given the timing, and it was confusing and seemed a silly consolation that you had taken on such a pretty nursemaid. Of course, the body of your letter made matters clear, and I apologize to you for my suspicion. But it really is a very lovely ensemble of people in these pictures, and they can make one forget for a time all of the terrible things that are part and parcel of living.

I have the fondest memories of Wolkenstein. If I'm not mistaken, your future husband visited us there, and I gave him his first lessons in mushroom hunting in the forest. But I'm suddenly unsure; it was most probably on Lake Carezza. Better ask him; my head is already 73 years old. In any case, I wish you as wonderful a time up there as it is possible to have in the Dolomites. Please convey my greetings to the Geisler Peaks along with Jetti and Edith.

Warmly, your Freud

21. (in same envelope as 20)

Dear Doctor,
I thank you for your kind offer, i.e., I accept it gladly. We hope to arrive at the Schneewinkellehen on the 17th or the 18th, and because it makes

---

39 Edith, her second daughter, was born on May 23, 1928.

no sense for me to smuggle my store of Hiestrich Half Coronas into Germany,[40] I will be very pleased to receive a few boxes of them and of the Calidai soon. H. has a shop in Berlin; I was there with Eitingon once. My other wishes, more difficult to fulfill, are for a not-too-hot summer, a well-behaved prosthesis that allows me to prolong my next visit to Berlin, peace and quiet among friends, and other such good things. I also have well-wishes for others, among them you and yours.

Warmly,
Your Freud

[Addressed to:]
Herr and Frau Dr. H. Lampl
Berlin-Dahlem, Schumacherplatz 2

21a.
[An A4 sheet of paper and text in Jeanne's handwriting]
Between these several reunions in Tegel-Berlin and several brief visits to Vienna. J.L-d Gr.

22.
PROF. DR. FREUD, VIENNA IX., BERGGASSE 19
March 14, 1931

My dear Jeanne,
I hurry to provide you all of the information that you might need for your decision. In the main, I can't do anything, I can't even give you advice. Only you can judge what you expect from the continuation of your analysis and what it may mean to you in terms of what you must sacrifice for it. No one else can assess the amount of libido expended in the process. In addition, I am prejudiced because I would like to see you again.

There are two issues on my side: Berlin and my summer stay. Regarding I: It would make no sense for me to come to Berlin now or in the near future. Because my symptoms are not the result of the prosthesis, but the consequences of my last two surgeries, which, though held to be unnecessary were justified as a precaution and therefore performed, and their effect is now evident. The wound surface is changing, shrinks, and no

---

40 Gerhart Fichtner noted in an email (August 28, 2011), "I know that Freud mentions Hiestrich Half Corona cigars in his letter to Hans Lampl dated June 2, 1929. These were Hiestrich cigars made by the company Schwering & Hasse, in Lügde, Germany, which did business from 1919 to 1952. The same company also made J.C. Caldas brand cigars [Calidai?], which are also mentioned in the letter to Hans. It may well be that before the world economic crisis of 1929 these cigars were easier to get in Holland than in Germany." Another cigar company by the name of W. Hiestrich also made half coronas in Hamburg.

revision of the prosthesis can be considered until something approaching a definitive state has been arrived at. In high summer no one is available in Berlin, and if possible I want to avoid a trip to Berlin in the fall. The situation is as follows: Hans was correct when he advised me back then to choose Ernst and not Schröder.[41] Schröder is too busy, and one needs a lot of time with him. It sounds very ungrateful, but that's how it is. My relationship with him is on an immoral basis because he refuses payment. In the end, I cannot endure having him make efforts again and again on my behalf. So I will try in Vienna to see whether the new prosthesis might be made by the intelligent and very obliging Dr. Weinmann. If that fails, I will approach Prof. Ernst, but that would have to wait for the winter.

Regarding II: Work on the prosthesis requires that I spend the summer in Vienna. We are in negotiations regarding a house in Salmannsdorf. I do not do it gladly. But it has the advantage that I can live in a garden earlier than usual, in May already. But the dentist isn't the only one I'm dependent on; as I realized last year, I'm also tied to an internist.[42] My choices are fewer each year; the path that remains open ever narrower. – So that's my situation, and I don't expect that you will find them enticing. But perhaps they will make your decision easier.

With warm greetings for you, your husband, and daughters,
Your Freud

[Addressed to:]
Frau Dr. Jeanne Lampl-de Groot
Berlin-Dahlem, Schumacherplatz 2

23.
PROF. DR. FREUD, VIENNA IX., BERGGASSE 19
May 20, 1931

My dear Jeanne,
First, I want to thank you, Hans, and the young ladies for your telegram.[43] That saves me a bit of official printed matter.

---

41 Hermann Schröder, who lived in Berlin, was a physician who treated Freud in November 1929. It is possible that Jeanne had visited him there as she wrote "a few . . . meetings in Tegel-Berlin" in her notes. The precise reports written by Dr. Pichler about more than 20 surgical procedures that Freud underwent from 1923 until his death in 1939, and the names of the physicians and colleagues who were present are extant thanks to Freud's personal physician Max Schur. They are reprinted in full in Appendix B (Surgical Notes) in Jones, E. (1957). Op. cit., pp. 468–495).
42 As a result of angina pectoris, which he was then experiencing for the first time.
43 On the occasion of Freud's 75th birthday.

In the matter of your analytic after-harvest or follow-up analysis, there is one point that we must set aside as uncertain and incalculable, that is, my capacity to take you on in the summer. It seems, however, that I should be able to pull myself together again. I am currently giving four sessions, and I am gaining weight, and the like. Two other matters should naturally be taken for granted, namely that I gladly take you on, and that I am in agreement with all financial suggestions. Plans such as the one you mentioned previously, to come in June and after 7 to 8 weeks of work continue in September, need not be discussed. I have nothing against the interruption; it would not impede your work, but the difficulty is that my working conditions will not be changed in June, i.e., as previously I will have five sessions. The first departure will be in July, and I don't know whether it will be in the beginning or middle, and because of my previous backlog I cannot send anyone away prematurely. I will certainly be freer in August and September, but I cannot predict the extent. The Princess has long been announced, but for when? and for how long? I have long promised Marianne Kris,[44] my adoptive daughter, to take her on as soon as I have time. In addition, a friendship analysis[45] is currently taking place, which awaits continuation. But only the Princess would take priority over you. You see that I am not rejecting your project as unfeasible; I'm simply drawing your attention to the necessary changes and unavoidable uncertainties. What do you have to say in response?

With warm greetings,
Your Freud

[Addressed to:]
Frau Dr. Jeanne Lampl-de Groot
Berlin-Dahlem, Schumacherplatz 2

24.
PROF. DR. FREUD, VIENNA IX., BERGGASSE 19
May 29, 1931

Dear Jeanne,
I have no objections to August 10. Let's leave it at that and hope that nothing gets in the way.

44 Marianne Kris, née Rie (1900–1980) was a psychiatrist and psychoanalyst, the daughter of the pediatrician Dr. Oscar Rie, who was a friend of the family and treated Freud's children. She introduced Ernst Kris to Freud. Both later underwent psychoanalytic training and were involved in theory development. They initially lived in Vienna but were later forced to emigrate to New York, where they settled in 1940 after spending two years in London. Both published many studies under their own names. Marianne and Ernst Kris were lifelong close friends of the Lampl-de Groots.
45 The word Freud uses is *Freundschaftsanalyse*. It is hard to know exactly what he meant given the lack of context.

Warmly,
Your Freud

[Addressed to:]
Frau Dr. Jeanne Lampl-de Groot
<u>Berlin-Dahlem</u>, Schumacherplatz 2

25.
PROF. DR. FREUD, VIENNA IX., BERGGASSE 19
July 18, 1931

My dear Jeanne,
I am very sorry to hear what is going on with little Edith.[46] I hope for a rapid recovery. Of course, we will postpone our arrangements until she is completely well. We can always continue again then. You will understand that I am not too worried about filling my time with analyses. Of course, with more leisure time I could do something else.
With warm wishes for all of you,
Your Freud

[Addressed to:]
Frau Dr. Jeanne Lampl-de Groot
<u>Berlin-Dahlem</u>, Schumacherplatz 2

26.
PROF. DR. FREUD, VIENNA IX., BERGGASSE 19
[handwritten:] XVIII Khevenhullerstr 6.
August 11, 1931

Dear Jeanne,
I must inform you of a change in my circumstances that will certainly interest you and Hans. Worn down by many years of torture, I have given in to Ruth Br.'s urgings.[47] She has learned that the renowned Harvard dentist Prof. Kazanjian is in Europe and I've given permission to have him invited to Vienna to make a prosthesis for me, although this attempt is associated with an extraordinary monetary expense. He began work on me yesterday, four hours in the morning and two hours in the afternoon.

---

46 In a June 4, 2011 email from Edith Lampl-Berkovits wrote: "I seem to remember that it was the onset of epiphysiolysis [Salter-Harris fracture] in my arm."
47 Ruth Mack Brunswick (1897–1946) was an American physician who began analysis with Freud in 1922. She later became a friend of the Freud family. In Jeanne's letters to her parents she is still referred to as Blumgart, the name of her then husband.

It was simply not possible for me to take more than two treatments that day. He is going to stay until the last week of August, and naturally he has first claim to my time. So, I must prepare you for the eventuality that you may not have daily sessions this month. I don't know, but I must assume the possibility, and I would like you to take that into consideration as well.

I am happy that the little one recovered so quickly, and I hope that all of you are well in the lovely Dolomites.

Warmly,
Your Freud

[Addressed to:]
Express
Frau Dr. Jeanne Lampl de Groot
Hotel de Brais, Villabassa, (Dolomites) Italy

26a
[Enclosure: handwritten letter from Jeanne Lampl-de Groot:]
Follow-up analysis from mid-August to mid-November 1931.

27.
PROF. DR. FREUD, VIENNA IX., BERGGASSE 19
November 15, 1931

My dear Jeanne,
I was just in the process of writing you a card which was supposed to contain nothing more than a big ?, when your first letter arrived with the good news, and before I could respond, your second letter. Of course, I hope to hear more from you, and I expectantly await reports about your mother in The Hague.

I myself have been fairly ill for the past 10 days with a stomach-intestinal revolution, and I even had to interrupt an analysis session in the middle because of a colonic spasm. Everything is functioning again, but my stomach is still sensitive and in need of care.

Jette's little story is charming. Why is it that with humans the buds are always so much more gratifying than the blossoms?

This question leads to the next topic. Given what we were able to offer it, your magnificent orchid apparently did not find its native East India. It deteriorated so badly that we asked Frl. Dr. Fürth to take it back again.

With warm greetings and wishes for all of you,
Your Freud

[Addressed to:]
Frau Dr. Jeanne Lampl-de Groot
Berlin-Dahlem, Schumacherplatz 2

28.
PROF. DR. FREUD, VIENNA IX., BERGGASSE 19
November 29, 1931

My dear Jeanne,

I know that I have not responded to you in a long while. The time did not pass without interruptions. I myself suffered in multiple ways, and we were all very preoccupied with Marianne Kris's newborn daughter's dangerous illness – *melena neonatorum*.[48] The child has now been saved by a blood transfusion, and I am well enough to be able to write again. And today is Sunday.

You guessed correctly why I wrote you so cautiously; I had feared domestic letter censorship. Now that you have reassured me about that, I gladly tell you that I share your hope for Hans's complete recovery. Only the sharp differentiation between the normal and foolish states is unfamiliar to me.[49] I very eagerly await further news.

You know about Martin's visit to Berlin.[50] In these days, in other words, I have three healthy and capable sons in the city, and not one of them can earn a heller.[51] Lively times.

I wish to thank Hans for the effort he made to procure the cigars for me. Unfortunately, they are so hard that I can't smoke them, the one type not at all, now and again one of the others. Perhaps don't mention this to him at all.

I ask that you act as a financial intermediary in December. Max's address (210 marks) is Neuer Wall 54.[52] I hope to hear from you very soon, and send greetings.

Warmly,

Your Freud

[Addressed to:]
Frau Dr. Jeanne Lampl-de Groot
<u>Berlin-Dahlem</u>, Schumacherplatz 2

---

48 Black, tarry feces caused by the digestion of blood in the gastrointestinal tract, not uncommon in infants.

49 It remains unclear what this is about, in later letters as well. One might speculate about how complex the relationship "in a threesome" must have been. The members of the Berkovits-Lampl family always experienced their father and grandfather as a caring, loving, humorous person (verbal communication).

50 Martin (1889–1967) was Freud's eldest son. He was a jurist, and after 1932 director of the Internationaler Psychoanalytischer Verlag. He emigrated to London in 1938.

51 An Austrian coin; the equivalent of saying they can't earn a red cent.

52 Max Halberstadt (1882–1940) had his photographic studio at Neuer Wall 54, Hamburg (May 4, 2015 e-mail from Regine Lockot).

29.
PROF. DR. FREUD, VIENNA IX., BERGGASSE 19
December 2, 1931

My dear Jeanne,

I am acting in accordance with your wish, and will keep your information confidential, including from Anna. But, reluctantly, I do not feel justified in hiding from you that these bouts worry me greatly, and that their intensity seems to far exceed what one would think likely from neurosis. I can imagine, and study on myself, just how energetically one rebels against such abominable possibilities,[53] but my worry for you predominates. I want you to open at least a modest space in your thinking about this calamity, and will thus be motivated to caution and a cool mistrust in addition to hope and love. I expect that you will be able to do so. Not every wife could.

You should also discuss this symptom with Sachs.[54] He isn't a doctor and will be unable to detect anything psychotic. I don't have any positive suggestions; in this matter I rely on you. But shouldn't you take someone really expert into your confidence in secret?

Please send me news soon. Is this perhaps (pre-)senile pessimism?

With warm wishes,

Your Freud

[Addressed to:]
Frau Dr. Jeanne Lampl-de Groot
Berlin-Dahlem, Schumacherplatz 2

30.
PROF. DR. FREUD, VIENNA IX., BERGGASSE 19
December 8, 1931

My dear Jeanne,

I am glad to hear your hopeful news. However, nothing appears decided. I have nothing to add to your discussion of the situation. If you think it expedient to come to Vienna over Christmas, I am available for you. I not only have four days completely free (24th–27th), but fewer sessions after that as well. You won't have to leave the house without good reason.

Thank you for delivery of the money!

---

53 It seems that Jeanne was very worried about Hans's psychic condition, and apparently feared psychiatric decompensation. This could explain Freud's fairly unusual advice, namely to take up contact with his analyst.
54 Hans Lampl was in psychoanalysis with Hanns Sachs.

Warmly,
Your Freud

[Addressed to:]
Frau Dr. Jeanne Lampl-de Groot
<u>Berlin-Dahlem</u>, Schumacherplatz 2

31.
PROF. DR. FREUD, VIENNA IX., BERGGASSE 19
December 17, 1931

My dear ones,
All of your small wishes can easily be satisfied because of the Christmas vacation. I am glad that you are all well, and I expect your final opinion. Sachs can visit me during his stay here.
With warm greetings,
Your Freud

[Addressed to:]
Herr and Frau Dr. H. Lampl
<u>Berlin-Dahlem</u>, Schumacherplatz 2

32.
PROF. DR. FREUD, VIENNA IX., BERGGASSE 19
January 17, 1932

My dear Jeanne,
I hope that your prolonged silence means only that everything is taking its desired course, and that you feel freed again, that Hans has worked diligently on his cure,[55] and that the children are well. I hope that I am not erring in these presumptions.

Eitingon was here yesterday to take part in cleaning out the Verlag. It seems that we have succeeded, although at great expense, which is necessary in order to pay Storfer's[56] personal debts, and to convince him to give up his position. His mismanagement has ruined everything. As important as he was as an editor and intellectual leader, his foolishness, disorder, and megalomania have had a terrifying effect on the business. Martin is replacing him as business manager; only when we have gotten rid of

---

55 Freud uses the word *cure* in other places as well when he means psychoanalysis.
56 Albert Josef Storfer (1888–1944) was the managing director of the Internationaler Psychoanalytischer Verlag from 1925 to 1932 (Jones, E. [1957]. Op. cit., p. 111).

Storfer will it become clear whether the Verlag can avoid a settlement and can continue with the necessary limitations.

At the same time, I have begun the battle against Reich[57] and Fenichel,[58] the Bolshevist attackers. My next intention is to change the editorial staff and move it to Vienna. But don't say anything about it. My stomach is all right again, which has improved my general sense of well-being. The prosthesis is not making any progress.

A brief article on the acquisition of fire in *Imago I* (1932)[59] will certainly interest you.

With warm greetings,
Your Freud

[Addressed to:]
Frau Dr. Jeanne Lampl-de Groot
Berlin-Dahlem, Schumacherplatz 1 [!]

33.
PROF. DR. FREUD, VIENNA IX., BERGGASSE 19
February 6, 1932

Dear Jeanne,

I was very pleased with your letters, their content, and the mood to which they attest, and I remain firm in the hope that the events will not put you to the test too severely. That you had to experience such unpleasantries from a patient whom I referred to you annoyed me greatly, but could not be predicted. This will not prevent me in similar circumstances.

Anna recovered quickly in Semmering; too quickly, actually, as I had hoped that she would have remained longer. It is now the fashion to get the grippe[60] again after a brief interval.

---

57 Wilhelm Reich (1897–1957) was initially a respected psychoanalyst, but became increasingly estranged from Freud both personally and politically (Jones, E. [1957]. Op. cit., pp. 166, 191).

58 Otto Fenichel (1897–1946) was a Viennese psychoanalyst and lecturer at the Berlin Psychoanalytical Institute. From 1934 until his forced emigration to the United States in 1938 he worked as a training analyst in Prague. He was very engaged in the social and political events of the day. In a letter dated January 9, 1932, to Max Eitingon, Freud accused Reich and Fenichel of using the psychoanalytical journals for Bolshevist propaganda. See Freud, S. & Eitingon, M. (2004). *Briefwechsel 1906–1939*. Ed. Michael Schröter. Tübingen: edition diskord, p. 778.

59 Freud, S. (1932). "The Acquisition and Control of Fire." In *Standard Edition*, vol. XXII. London: Hogarth, pp. 187–193.

60 A non-specific term that described the flu or flu-like symptoms.

We will probably be able to maintain the Verlag, i.e., I myself am prepared to bear the great debt that it will entail. Contributions from Eitingon, Brill,[61] and Jackson[62] have been supportive.

As you know, the matter concerning Reich is in Bernfeld's[63] hands. I am seriously considering replacing Fenichel with a Viennese editor; it will also be more congenial and cheaper. Everywhere revolution and disorder; a new order is required.

I am not very satisfied either with the prosthesis or my general health. The winter is not good for old people.

With warm greetings, especially for your big daughter,

Your Freud

[Addressed to:]
Frau Dr. Jeanne Lampl-de Groot
Berlin-Dahlem, Schumacherplatz 2

34.
PROF. DR. FREUD, VIENNA IX., BERGGASSE 19
February 13, 1932

Dear Jeanne,

Your cigars are good and mild, easy to smoke, and make me regret that I have to monitor my use so carefully. I hope that your news, too, remains good.

Martin now has the Verlag firmly under control. We hope to save it. I will soon write you more about certain plans that I am making for its future. Anna appears to have recovered well, but other than that one hears only bad news.

---

61 Abraham Arden Brill (1874–1948) was an American psychoanalyst, president of the American Psychoanalytic Association and vice president of the International Psychoanalytic Association. He played an important role in the publication of psychoanalytic literature, and in the financial support of the Internationaler Psychoanalytischer Verlag, as well as in the discussions around lay analysis.

62 Edith Jackson (1895–1977) was an American child psychiatrist who was in training analysis with Freud and was trained at the Vienna Institute. In 1937 she and Dorothy Burlingham founded and financed the Jackson Kindergarten for poor children from Vienna – precursor of the Hampstead War Nurseries in London, which later became the Anna Freud National Centre for Children and Families. The Anna Freud Centre remains an internationally recognized research and training center. Jackson later became a professor of pediatrics and psychiatry at the Yale School of Medicine.

63 Siegfried Bernfeld (1892–1953) was born in Lviv (formerly Lemberg, Galicia, today in western Ukraine. He studied biology and psychology in Vienna, worked there as a psychoanalyst from 1922 to 1925, and after 1925 in Berlin. Bernfeld was asked to write an editorial response to Reich's problematic paper in the *Internationale Zeitschrift für Psychoanalyse*.

With warm greetings for you, Hans, and the young ladies,
Your Freud

[Addressed to:]
Frau Dr. Jeanne Lampl-de Groot
Berlin-Dahlem, Schumacherplatz 2

35.
PROF. DR. FREUD, VIENNA IX., BERGGASSE 19
February 18, 1932

Dear Jeanne,

Don't worry about writing me as often as you feel the need. I don't currently detect anything threatening in your news. The interval since the last fit has been quite long, and the fact that his jealousy finds an outlet in me directly is perhaps unavoidable in light of its course. The process that has begun obviously cannot be interrupted, but rather must come to its natural conclusion. It is our hope that in the meantime he will be caught by the analytic process, so that it passes without lasting damage. Regrettable is the damage caused to your feelings for him, which may be restored given a good outcome.

I am contemplating writing "New Lectures"[64] during the summer as a supplement to the introduction, assuming of course, Destiny's grace. I may perhaps need literature suggestions for several chapters. May I count on you for this? But keep this matter confidential. Here, only Anna and Martin know about it.

Your cigars are the best and mildest that I could wish for. Unfortunately, Eitingon now neglects my supply, or perhaps his travel opportunities are less frequent. At some point, let me know how much money I still have with you in credit.

With warmest greetings,
Your Freud

[Addressed to:]
Frau Dr. Jeanne Lampl-de Groot
Berlin-Dahlem, Schumacherplatz 2

---

64 *New Introductory Lectures on Psychoanalysis.* In his preface, Freud wrote that in contrast to the *Introductory Lectures on Psychoanalysis* from the years 1915 to 1917, these new lectures had never actually been given. "My age had in the meantime absolved me from the obligation of giving expression to my membership of the University (which was in any case a peripheral one) by delivering lectures; and a surgical operation had made speaking in public impossible for me." He characterized the New Lectures as "continuations and supplements," to the previous series, which fall into three groups that contain "fresh treatments," "critical revisions" of previous themes, and "true extensions." Of interest is also his statement that "This time once again it has been my chief aim to make no sacrifice to an appearance of being simple, complete or rounded-off, not to disguise problems and not to deny the existence of gaps and uncertainties." In *Standard Edition*, vol. XXII. London: Hogarth, pp. 5–6.

36.
PROF. DR. FREUD, VIENNA IX., BERGGASSE 19
March 2, 1932

My dear Jeanne,
I thank God for your good news.[65] (As an interjection, we really can't do without God.) I have the impression that it signifies a decisive turn, and potential fluctuations won't ruin anything anymore. If that's the way it is, you need not worry about your feelings about the future.

I thank you for so conscientiously taking care of the money matters. It seems that the Verlag has a chance to survive this most difficult period. Martin, who is very engaged, has received a lengthier moratorium from his creditors. Naturally, it depends on whether sales increase in Germany. If that doesn't happen, we will have to close our doors again. But then at least in an honorable fashion. My "New Lectures" are not an inner need of mine; they are meant to help the Verlag. It's a secret about them, don't forget. Even Eitingon doesn't know. I really want to hand the editorship of *Imago*[66] over to Wälder[67] and Kris,[68] but only after Storfer's departure, which will free up editorial space at the Verlag. As far as the Journal[69] is concerned, I will take Eitingon's suggestion to wait until Radó's[70] intentions are known. It is very hard for me to still my dislike of Fenichel, even though he has turned away from Reich.

You were completely right to call Horney[71] to account. It is peculiar that Alexander[72] thinks so well of her too. He looks forward to her collabora-

---

65 Apparently, Jeanne's worries about her husband's psychological balance had abated.
66 *Imago* was a psychoanalytic journal founded in 1912 by Hans Sachs and Otto Rank, both non-physicians. It attempted to popularize the use of psychoanalysis in the humanities and arts.
67 Robert Wälder (1900–1967) and Ernst Kris published *Imago* from 1932 to 1938.
68 Ernst Kris (1900–1957), husband of Marianne Kris-Rie, was an art historian and psychoanalyst. He emigrated to London in 1938, and to New York in 1940. With Anna Freud and others, he played an important role as cofounder and coeditor of the annual *Psychoanalytic Study of the Child*. From its founding in 1945 up to the present time, it has published a selection of theoretical and technical papers about child analysis and development. Kris was also coeditor of Freud's *Gesammelte Werke* (the German edition of his *Collected Works*).
69 *Internationale Zeitschrift für Psychoanalyse*.
70 At this point, Sándor Radó (1890–1972) was in the United States, and was uncertain whether he would return to Vienna. He did not.
71 Karen Horney (1885–1952) was born in Hamburg and studied medicine in Freiburg and Berlin. She began her training analysis in 1910 under Karl Abraham and was a founding member of the Berlin Institute. In a large number of papers and articles, she refocused the psychoanalytic viewpoint to that of the psychological development of women. By doing so, she created room for a much broader spectrum of developmental possibilities, including female homosexuality. Horney emigrated to the United States in 1932, where she joined Franz Alexander, who had emigrated in 1920. He invited her to become associate director at the Chicago Psychoanalytic Institute. After two years, she moved to New York, where in 1941 she founded and became dean of the American Institute of Psychoanalysis. Later she resigned from the AIP and taught at the New York Medical College. Horney continued practicing as a psychiatrist until her death in 1952.
72 Franz Alexander (1891–1964), born in Budapest, was a physician and psychoanalyst, and a lecturer at the Berlin Institute. In 1930 he became the first professor of psychoanalysis at the University of Chicago.

tion and hopes soon to dissuade her of her opposition. I know her only as malevolent and as an intriguer.

We got the house in Pötzleinsdorf again and hope to move over there during the second half of May. The garden did me much good last year. I have little reason to be satisfied with the prosthesis, but this time the blame lies more with an infectious catarrh, which I got at the same time as Anna, and which lingers with me as much as it has with her. Furthermore, it is apparently necessary to surgically revise the scar once again, which has been postponed only on account of the catarrh. But it is supposed to be done next Monday. Pichler thinks it won't be horrible.

With warm greetings to all of you!

Your Freud

[Addressed to:]
Frau Dr. Jeanne Lampl-de Groot
Berlin-Dahlem, Schumacherplatz 2

37.
PROF. DR. FREUD, VIENNA IX., BERGGASSE 19
March 19, 1932

My dear Jeanne,
I am very happy about the report concerning your own well-being. What you write about Hans requires no change in our expectations; the increase in the intervals between one attack and the next remains what is important in terms of prognosis and is of course favorable.

My surgery and the week thereafter were really much less horrible than usual. During the second week, which is now coming to an end, the pain was stronger, and together with my stomach and intestinal problems made for a very uncomfortable time. Healing seems to be proceeding more quickly since removal of the stitches, although I cannot declare myself to have been restored, and in addition, things happen daily that shouldn't.

Thomas Mann's[73] visit day before yesterday was a very pleasant experience. He is a charming man and after the first five minutes we were able to talk intimately.

---

73 Thomas Mann (1875–1955) wrote about Freud on various occasions. His essay, which he sent to Freud, titled "Die Stellung Freuds in der modernen Geistesgeschichte" [Freud's Position in the History of Modern Culture], appeared in 1929. It was published in English in Mann, T. (1933). *Past Masters and Other Papers*. New York: Knopf. Freud acknowledged the essay in a letter, but made several gentle corrections to Mann's text. (Mann, T. [1974]. *Thomas Mann: Gesammelte Werke in Dreizehn Bänden* [Thomas Mann: Collected Works in Thirteen Volumes], vol. X, 2nd revised edition. Frankfurt am Main: S. Fischer Verlag, pp. 256–280). In 1931, on the occasion of Freud's 75th birthday, Mann wrote "Ritter zwischen Tod und Teufel" [Knight between the Devil and Death], vol. X, pp. 465–467. On

Martin is working diligently at the Verlag; Ernstl is making an excellent impression on us. We are all tired of winter; we will supposedly be enjoying the spring in Pötzleinsdorf in two months.

You will be warmly welcomed by us whenever you come for a visit. This time you haven't written anything about the children. Apparently they are doing very well.

With warmest greetings,
Your Freud

[Addressed to:]
Frau Dr. Jeanne Lampl-de Groot
Berlin-Dahlem, Schumacherplatz 2

38.
PROF. DR. FREUD, VIENNA IX., BERGGASSE 19
March 25, 1932

My dear Jeanne,

It is of course unwelcome to hear that this time Hans has remained in his state for so long, and that Sachs is taking a break just now. During such a time the patient should actually be taking a holiday from the site of his difficulties. Is that not possible in his case?

I am almost past the pain and functional impediments. Because these surgeries were undertaken not to improve function, but rather as a precaution, there is, so to speak, no gain from having had it. Only the question, when is the next one? The whole thing is really uncomfortable, and the certainty that I would be able to do the work that I have set myself during the following months is, of course, not overly great. Up to now I have been able to make few preparations.

To view our nearest and dearest as products of nature like everything else, and to accept their particular destinies is perhaps even more difficult than to accept one's own destiny. No, the pleasure principle is not satisfied in life. One can always gain a certain foothold in oneself, others vanish so easily from our view.

I would like to send my warmest Easter greetings; if only it weren't still so icy and un-springlike. But with undiminished warmth,
Your Freud

[Addressed to:]
Frau Dr. Jeanne Lampl-de Groot
Berlin-Dahlem, Schumacherplatz 2

Freuds 80th birthday in 1936 he delivered the ceremonial address titled "Freud und die Zukunft" [Freud and the Future], vol. IX, pp. 478–501.

39.
PROF. DR. FREUD, VIENNA IX., BERGGASSE 19
April 12, 1932

My dear Jeanne,

I am satisfied by your news, which is good in all important respects. Their minor fluctuations may well be grounded in the normal course of things; you, however, appear to think that they are residual manifestations of the neurosis. We will see. From the photographs it is increasingly difficult for me to distinguish Jetti and Edith, but I think you will succeed in that.

Martin has not yet overcome all of the problems with the Verlag, but that will undoubtedly happen soon. Storfer will be leaving on the 24th of this month, not without causing unpleasantries to the very end. I won't be able to do anything about the editorship of *Imago* until Storfer has left; as long as Radó is still undecided, nothing can be done with the Journal. My circular letter to the associations regarding aid for the Verlag will be coming back from the printer today. You and Hans will receive a joint copy.

We are planning to move to Poetzleinsdorf on May 15. Perhaps this year we'll have a little spring. All of the effects of the last surgery are past; the prosthesis is working more or less. I want to enjoy in peace the interval until the next surgery, which I think will be necessary.

The unpleasant news, which is probably new to you as well, arrived in a letter from my wife, who is in Berlin. Eitingon is confined to bed and cannot move his left arm. He foresees several weeks of rest. His wife speaks of nicotine poisoning, obviously a pretext. What's behind this? Because they are keeping this illness a secret, I have to ask you not to do anything to spread the news. The coincidence with the financial collapse is hardly accidental; it increases the gravity of the situation. Even apart from this, his constitution does not seem the healthiest, neither in physical nor emotional respects.

We are now waiting to hear what my wife has to say about her visit with you.

With warm greetings,
Your Freud

[Addressed to:]
Frau Dr. Jeanne Lampl-de Groot
Berlin-Dahlem, Schumacherplatz 2

40.
PROF. DR. FREUD, VIENNA IX., BERGGASSE 19
April 17, 1932

My dear Jeanne,

I thank you for everything: letters, news, manuscript, and cigars. I cannot tell you as much about the next to last as you hope for.[74] That is the consequence of a peculiarity that is now difficult to change. For a long time after I have worked on something it becomes alien to me and inaccessible. During the summer holidays I will have to revisit the topic that the two of us worked on. At present I have gotten at least an impression of your work. The favorable first: I noted the wealth of ideas that you justifiably draw on. Obviously, a great deal must be done theoretically with the conceptualization of the two drives, especially the death drive; one simply has to take it seriously and find out how to deal with it. The idea that narcissism is necessarily used in the ego to neutralize self-destruction is splendid; attempts to pursue such an equilibrium of drives is surely hopeless. I don't know how much time I will be able to spend on this during the summer. I don't currently have an assessment of the whole, although I have two objections. The first relates to the description in which what is new is not sufficiently distinguished from the known, nor the theoretical from observation. The second is the justification for the title, because the problems relating to passive determinacy seem to be touched on only at one end, and not at the most important.

You should rewrite the article in any case and complete it in the process. It is good that you won't be hearing from me again about this because in matters of production one should be subject to [no][75] influences if possible, at most receiving encouragement and now and again an exhortation.

If you really need a follow-up to your analysis, I am more prepared to do so than you might expect. During the summer I will probably have no sessions, and no new appointments have been made for the fall. Of my previous cases, perhaps three will come again. It is no wonder that people no longer come to me. If only it were completely unimportant to me.

---

74 This concerns the 1933 paper "Zu den Problemen der Weiblichkeit" [Problems of Femininity] (in *Internationale Zeitschrift für Psychoanalyse*, 19, 385–415, and in *The Psychoanalytic Quarterly*, 2, 489–518). Jeanne added the following to the English translations: "Perhaps this paper is partly a youthful sin; perhaps I should have changed more than only a few of the formulations. Be that as it may, I have decided to publish it with only slight differences in wording because I myself cannot reject it altogether, though I am quite aware of its speculative side and am prepared to abandon it whenever different and better hypotheses are presented." (Lampl-de Groot, J. [1985]. *Man and Mind. Collected Papers of Jeanne Lampl-de Groot*. New York: International Universities Press, pp. 12–32).

75 Freud omitted the word *no*; possibly a sign of his ambivalence?

On Tuesday, when my wife returns, she will tell me about her visit with you.

Warmly,

Your Freud

P.S. I'm sure you've received the circular letter by now!

[Addressed to:]

Frau Dr. Jeanne Lampl-de Groot

Berlin-Dahlem, Schumacherplatz 2

41.

PROF. DR. FREUD, VIENNA IX., BERGGASSE 19

April 24, 1932

My dear Jeanne,

First, in answer to your inquiry. We anticipate moving out there at Pentecost, and at the moment I will have only three regular sessions, and so there will be enough time for you.

You see, even my few remarks about your paper bothered you. There is also too much subjective in it, which you could not guess at. For me, something floats – completely literally – over the passive drive goals, a formulation of the problem that I sometimes almost catch a glimpse of, but which then becomes shrouded again. When I read your paper, I had it again at that moment, and then when your descriptions didn't hit it, I was distracted from appreciating it and jotted down what I now recognize as having been unfair. Now I'm fumbling around in the dark again; I have no way of knowing whether my approach will yield anything, perhaps in the free time I have in Poetzleinsdorf, if at all. But I think, coming back to your paper, that it would be very unjust if you became discouraged and withdrew your interest from working out and setting down your thoughts, because what I have seen is rich in content and very promising.

My wife enjoyed her stay in Berlin very much, even though not everything that she saw was wonderful. The times are actually terrible, and there is no guarantee of a more tolerable future. The evident general concern for the fate of the Verlag does me good. I thank you for your good intentions. Hopefully, Eitingon will soon be in a position to initiate deliberations in the Berlin group. Martin is available for all information.

As a result of your encouragement, Bernfeld will receive a copy of the paper that he so admired.

Your stamps are always welcome; even the duplicates are usable by young collectors.

Hopefully you will have another lengthy rest period with regard to the domestic (I obviously meant Hansian[76]) neurosis. My reserve regarding your paper does not mean that I wouldn't want to read it in a revised form. Perhaps I can borrow even more.

Warm greetings,
from Your Freud

[Addressed to:]
Frau Dr. Jeanne Lampl-de Groot
Berlin-Dahlem, ~~Allensteinerstr. 26~~
[in different handwriting:] Schumacherplatz 2

42.
[Postcard]
PROF. DR. FREUD, VIENNA IX., BERGGASSE 19
May 8, 1932

Dear Jeanne,
I will be brief in my thanks because I will see you soon.
Moving the editing to Vienna is as good as a closed matter. This week the final discussions with the new men.
Warmly,
Your Freud

[Address:]
Herr and Frau
Dr. Hans Lampl
<u>Berlin-Dahlem</u>, Schumacherplatz 2

43.
[Postcard]
Vienna, May 9, 1932
Additionally:
The orchid arrived safely this morning and is unbelievably beautiful.

[Address:]
Frau Dr. Jeanne Lampl de Groot
<u>Berlin-Dahlem</u>, Schumacherplatz 2

---

76 Freud is making an adjective out of Hans's name.

44.
PROF. DR. FREUD, VIENNA IX., BERGGASSE 19
June 18, 1932

Dear Jeanne,
Do not be surprised that you are now hearing from me so seldom, and don't let your urge to send me news be influenced by it. I am working on the Lectures,[77] and that requires an unbelievable amount of concentration, and is much more difficult than it used to be. One and a half are finished, except for the necessary revisions. I will have a good amount of time on the 27th of this month after my next-to-last patient has departed. Naturally, drive theory will be discussed; however, I don't have much new to say about it. The garden is lovely, and the weather often ideal.

It seems that everything is going well with you. Sachs's position in Boston now seems certain. It appears to me that Hans will decide to undergo analysis during the summer weeks. I heard that you had a scare with your mother-in-law, thankfully resolved. What did you find in Holland?

Do not overestimate your difficulties in the work. Part of that is certainly normal. I see it now in myself, how hard it is to master new material in scientific work. And even so, what I'm doing is mostly rumination. Of course, one can't quickly deal with the emanations of the elementary drives.

If you think you will need me, I am free for the entire summer.
With warm greetings,
Your Freud

[Addressed to:]
Frau Dr. Jeanne Lampl-de Groot
Berlin-Dahlem, Schumacherplatz 2

45.
PROF. DR. FREUD, VIENNA IX., BERGGASSE 19
July 3, 1932
[added in handwriting: Vienna] XVIII Khevenhüllerg[asse] 6

Dear Jeanne,
Sachs came to visit me, and we agreed on a favorable interpretation of the present situation. He thinks that Hans should definitely continue analysis during the summer weeks, and I think so too. Even more persuasive than Sachs's report, however, was a letter from Hans himself, completely

---

77 Freud, S. (1933 [1964]). "New Introductory Lectures on Psychoanalysis." *Standard Edition*, vol. XXII. London: Hogarth.

reasonable, not at all excessively overoptimistic, almost objective, as if it had been written by someone else. We know what fluctuations in affect are possible, but we must be glad for what has already been achieved. As always I am at your service *if* and *when* you need it.

How are you arranging things with my subsidies during the summer months while you are absent? And how much do I still have in credit with you? Oli[78] will be returning to Berlin in early August. The Dutch cigars are still the best for me, but I can't accept such quantities as gifts. Please subtract them from my credit. Eitingon, too, must be compensated for his expenses [for his days] at Berchtesgaden.[79]

I am deeply immersed in the Lectures, which are not easy for me, and I am sensitive to the many little disturbances. The work is possible only because I have so little to do, two sessions. I don't think I will discuss technique; the Lectures are not aimed at analysts. As of now I foresee six to eight Lectures.

I'm having a better time with the prosthesis; other than that, I don't want to be too demanding.

I wish you an undisturbed summer on your lovely mountain, which unfortunately I have not seen. We were in San Martino and Lake Carezza.

Warm greetings,
Your Freud

[Address:]
Signora Dr. Jeanne Lampl de Groot
Madonna di Campiglio
(Alto Adige) Italy, Hotel Campo

46.
PROF. DR. FREUD, VIENNA IX., BERGGASSE 19
July 15, 1932

My dear Jeanne,
The return of Hans's states of irritability are certainly vexing, and the fact that he keeps experiencing the same thing even when he has composed himself is not satisfactory. It is good that he is continuing with analysis. Perhaps the drops of water will hollow out the stone after all.[80] You may come when you wish. You know that I am quite free during real

78 Oliver (1891–1969), Freud's third child and second son, became an engineer. He emigrated to France in 1933 and to the United States in 1942.
79 At the congress held there.
80 Gutta cavat lapidem, non vi sed saepe cadendo: A drop of water hollows a stone, not with force but by falling often.

vacations. I am writing diligently, but am not finding it easy; my writing inhibitions may well be physiologically based. It annoys me every time I leave out words or put them in the wrong place. That never used to happen.

The draft of the last Lecture, about Weltanschauung,[81] is done; only a clean copy remains to be written out. The first two, the "Revision of the Dream Theory" and "Dreams and Occultism," are in their final form. Right now I'm working on the third one, "Dissection of the Personality," which is difficult.[82] I am contemplating a fourth, "Anxiety and Instinctual Life."[83] It is unclear what will follow thereafter, but what is clear is that I won't have finished the task in Poetzleinsdorf. Half of our summer here has already passed. It has been lovely up to now.

I am very happy that you are able to work so well, but do not confuse well with easily. Everything of this sort is difficult.

Serendipity brought Martin's family together with Oli and his family in Mallnitz.

With warm wishes for a lovely summer for you.

Your Freud.

[Address:]
Signora Dr. Jeanne Lampl de Groot
Madonna di Campiglio
Trento, Italy, Golf Hotel Campo

47.
PROF. DR. FREUD, VIENNA IX., BERGGASSE 19
July 30, 1932

My dear Jeanne,

The time of your move approaches; I am looking forward to seeing you again, even if only for a few days. Officially I should suggest to you that you spend this time in our guest room, which *very probably* will be unoccupied around August 15. I could not mention what might possibly keep you from accepting the offer.[84] If you dare, you are welcome; if you think

---

81 Freud, S. (1933). "New Introductory Lectures on Psycho-Analysis." Lecture XXXV in *Standard Edition*, vol. XXII. London: Hogarth, pp. 158–182.
82 Lectures XXIX, XXX, XXXI and XXXII, respectively, in Freud, S. (1933). Op. cit., pp. 7–30, 31–56, 57–80, 81–111.
83 Freud still was not clear about "Femininity" at this time. Here there is a connection with Jeanne, who was also examining femininity (Freud, S. [1933 (1964)]. "Femininity." Lecture XXXIII in *Standard Edition*, vol. XXII. London: Hogarth, pp. 112–135.
84 Here for the first time Freud broaches the problem of mixing treatment and personal relationships.

that this would provoke Hans, send some sort of excuse. I would like to make the decision for you in the positive, but I know too little of your circumstances.

It is a time of distressingly tense expectation in more than one respect, both in small and large circles. In the meantime, we're both working. I, too, am at least being diligent despite both minor complaints and treatments. Our weather seems to have been much milder than yours. On the 26th we spent a completely lovely half day at Hochrotherd.[85]

With warm greetings,
Your Freud

[Address:]
Frau Dr Jeanne Lampl-de Groot
Madonna di Campiglio
Trento Italy, Golf Hotel Campo

Figure 13 Jeanne, 1935.

85 Hochrotherd – sometimes abbreviated HRE – was a country house that Anna Freud and Dorothy Burlingham bought in the fall of 1931.

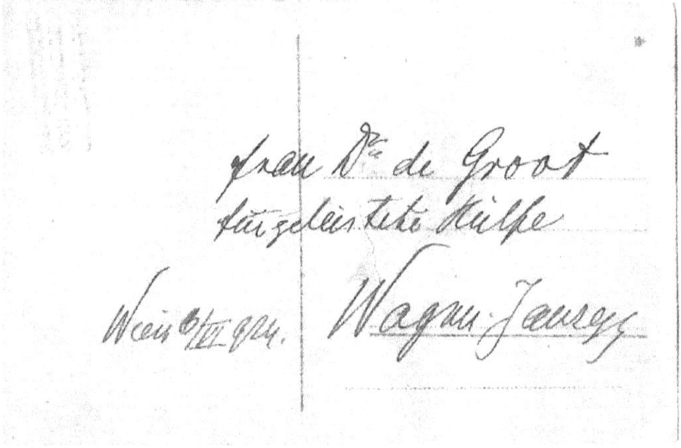

Figure 14 "Frau Dr. de Groot for assistance rendered. Vienna June 6, 1924, Wagner-Jauregg"; dedication on the back of the photo below from Jeanne's teacher in psychiatry.

Figure 15 Nobel laureate Julius Wagner-Jauregg, 1924.

Figure 16 Berlin, Villa Lampl, Architect Ernst Freud, 1927.

Figure 17 Berlin, 1931. Jeanne, Edith (left) and Henriëtte (right).
Photo: Hans Lampl

Figure 18 Berlin, Winter 1932. Henriëtte (left), Edith (right).

Photo: Walter Talbot, Berlin

Figure 19 Vienna, Pyrkergasse or Sternwartestrasse, 1934. From left to right: Edith, Jeanne, Henriëtte with Tattoun.

Figure 20 Jeanne at the founding of the Greek study group, 1948. Marie Bonaparte, Jeanne, Prince George of Greece.

Photo: Hans Lampl

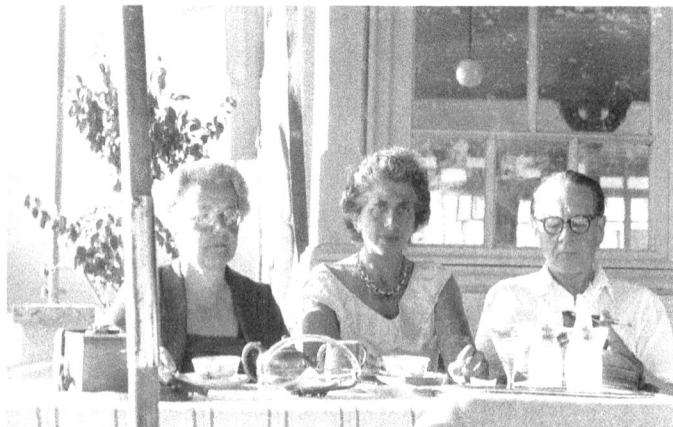

Figure 21 Jeanne with Dora and Heinz Hartmann, ca. 1960.

Photo: Hans Lampl

Figure 22 17th IPA Congress 1951, Amsterdam. Heinz Hartmann, Jeanne, Hans Lampl.

48.
PROF. DR. FREUD, VIENNA IX., BERGGASSE 19
September 8, 1932

Dear Jeanne,
Anna will be arriving only this evening, but Ruth confirmed to me that your lecture, the content of which would have found favor, suffered from the way in which you spoke.[86] Because you behaved the way you do in analysis and didn't notice that you were speaking so softly and were amazed that no one made you aware of it (Ruth says that people yelled "louder" to you several times), it occurs to me that you were self-punishing for your resistance in the analysis. Your performance signals your competition with me, and because of this naughtiness you were forced to subtract something from your success.
I was extremely happy about your good news regarding Hans. Hopefully it will stay like that, and then everything will be easier for you.
Warm greetings,
Your Freud

[Addressed to:]
Frau Dr. Jeanne Lampl-de Groot
Berlin-Dahlem, Schumacherplatz 2

49.
PROF. DR. FREUD, VIENNA IX., BERGGASSE 19
October 8, 1932

My dear Jeanne,
In the meantime you will have seen Anna and learned from her whatever is worth knowing. The latest is that day before yesterday Pichler performed another one of those small surgeries in my mouth that he considers necessary as a precaution, this time much more energetically than the last. But everything went well; I had wound pain only for three hours, and I tolerated all injections well. Today I'm going out; Monday I'll work again. Of course, there is no guarantee that this will be the last of its sort.
Your good news is very pleasing. Whether a deficit in his personality remains will not yet be clear.[87] In that case you would have to make up for it with an expansion in your own. I think you could do that.

---

86 Jeanne spoke at the Psychoanalytic Congress in Wiesbaden on November 4, 1932. Freud refers to her presentation here with an off-the-cuff interpretation in which he presents his own fantasies about her performance.
87 In classical psychiatry, it was believed that a personality could be changed after a psychotic break, especially in cases of schizophrenia.

After November 1 we will leave the rest of the 140 marks with you as a credit for cigars and the like. There have been no new patients, and none are in prospect. Ferenczi[88] has been diagnosed with pernicious anemia; we were almost prepared for worse. The liver treatment is very promising. But not nice in any case.

In your last photograph I noticed that Edith exhibits a completely new facial expression. Is that really the case?

Warm greetings,

Your Freud

[Addressed to:]
Frau Dr. Jeanne Lampl-de Groot
Berlin-Dahlem, Schumacherplatz 2

50.
PROF. DR. FREUD, VIENNA IX., BERGGASSE 19
October 23, 1932

My dear Jeanne,

Just a few lines so that our correspondence doesn't freeze up. I am always glad to get your news and descriptions.

Hans's last attack can really be described as a "fruste,"[89] and has good prospects. It amused me that I was right about Edith. Nothing much new here. I am well, still have wound pain from the last burning[90] on the 6th of this month. Five hours of work with little income and no prospects for more. Ruth is a very irregular patient and very hard to grasp given her organic complications.

Of the seven New Lectures, three have already been typeset and corrected.

As you perhaps already know, Ferenczi has pernicious anemia, but is recovering well with liver treatment. Our relations have been interrupted, but his doctor, Dr. Léos [Léoz] keeps me informed.[91]

Mathilde has recovered well after the x-ray storm.[92]

---

88 Sándor Ferenczi (1873–1933), a Hungarian psychiatrist, studied medicine in Vienna and opened a psychoanalytic practice in Budapest. He belonged to the first generation of analysts around Freud and is still respected for his critical scientific originality (see also Szecsödy, I. [2007]. "Sándor Ferenczi – the First Intersubjectivist." *The Scandinavian Psychoanalytic Review*, 30, 33–42).

89 *Forme fruste* is a diagnostic term in psychiatry. It describes a group of milder symptoms that do not fit into a specific clinical picture.

90 Freud is referring to the cauterization of blood vessels or cancerous tissue.

91 Another interesting indiscretion.

92 Radioactive treatment.

I send warm greetings to you all.
Your Freud

[Addressed to:]
Frau Dr. Jeanne Lampl-de Groot
<u>Berlin-Dahlem</u>, Schumacherplatz 2

51.
PROF. DR. FREUD, VIENNA IX., BERGGASSE 19
November 7, 1932

Dear Jeanne,

I'm naturally much more partial to unalloyed good news from you than what was in today's letter, but I agree with you completely that such incidents do not contradict the impression that a great change for the better has been achieved. One may hope that this residuum will fade. Do not worry about the necessity of a maternal attitude toward your husband; it was bound to occur sooner or later, though in your case it came too early.

After a not very pleasant week of grippe with fever, otitis, paracentesis,[93] etc., today I am taking up work again, limiting it from 2 to 5. Naturally I am not yet very strong, but I am human again. Thankfully, the other illnesses in the house were much milder. The Lectures will certainly be published before Christmas. If you *wish*, I will send you the edits beforehand, although it is no pleasure to read such scraps.

Many thanks for your conscientious money management throughout these many months. Use will easily be found for the rest of the 140 marks. I still have a good half of the Dutch cigars, and I assume that you subtracted them from my credit as well. If you decide to procure more, then the rest is taken care of.

At present, my desire to hold evening discussions is understandably not great. Wait to see what the future holds. It is lovely that you have established a firm foothold in your work.

Warm greetings to all.
Your Freud

[Addressed to:]
Frau Dr. Jeanne Lampl-de Groot
<u>Berlin-Dahlem</u>, Schumacherplatz 2

---

93 Surgical puncturing, in this case of the eardrum to treat a purulent ear infection.

52.
PROF. DR. FREUD, VIENNA IX., BERGGASSE 19
November 19, 1932

Dear Jeanne,
I've sent you the raw manuscript of the New Lectures.[94] Once you, and naturally Hans if he wishes, have read them, pass them along to Eitingon, but not too late as they are to be printed in early December.
I am not happy about your news.
Warmly, Your Freud

[Addressed to:]
Frau Dr. Jeanne Lampl-de Groot
Berlin-Dahlem, Schumacherplatz 2

53.
PROF. DR. FREUD, VIENNA IX., BERGGASSE 19
December 11, 1932

My dear Jeanne,
On Thursday I had another diathermy burn from Pichler. Boring, that the tissue doesn't want to calm down. Each time he says that what was removed was of a completely harmless character, but you know, if one had allowed it time, perhaps, etc. As always there was initially little pain and few symptoms, but after a few days the unpleasantness of the inflammatory reaction, and to not be able to chew, barely speak, and strangely, hardly write.
The book has been published. You were one of the first readers. This evening I will have a copy sent to you. For Christmas I will officially take only three days of vacation, Saturday to Monday. But whoever wishes will get more, and if you come to Vienna I will certainly have time for you. I was extraordinarily relieved that things are going well for you again.
I hope to get news from you before Christmas.
Warm greetings to you all,
Your Freud

[Addressed to:]
Frau Dr. Jeanne Lampl-de Groot
Berlin-Dahlem, Schumacherplatz 2

94 Freud, S. (1933 [1964]). "New Introductory Lectures on Psychoanalysis." In *Standard Edition*, vol. XXII. London: Hogarth.

54.
PROF. DR. FREUD, VIENNA IX., BERGGASSE 19
January 8, 1933

My dear Jeanne,

When your letter arrived Anna and I had just been ruminating over the same topic that you are thinking about: why all the people who are close to us are so *meschugge*.[95] No clear resolution can be found, but that's how it is. The couple who arrived recently, your friend Bernfeld and Suse P[aret] K[assirer],[96] appear to want to accomplish great things. I saw B. day before yesterday and P. arrived only yesterday. An equation with two unknowns. Their statements don't agree at all, the condition of both should probably be understood only as neurotic, and their analysis is too recent to reveal the key. He accused himself to me and condemned his actions as malicious, but seems not to have undertaken any corrective steps. Their statements are completely unreliable, contrived, exaggerated, and God knows what effect they strive for. How a sound analysis is to be conducted under these circumstances is completely unclear. Some *malheur* will certainly result from it. About that I can do nothing right now.

My wounds are slowly healing, but the end effect seems not very satisfactory. Future uncertain. You saw Martin in Berlin; he was completely enchanted by Jette.

We have both finally achieved insight into Hans's condition as never before. I think that the line of conduct that you have set yourself will prove appropriate. For the rest, continue to slave away. After three weeks of fog and black ice we finally had a moment of sunshine and temperatures above +/-0 degrees. I drive out almost daily, but with little pleasure in the outside world.

I am very glad to hear that the Berlin practice is beginning to pick up, and I send warm greetings,

Your Freud

[Addressed to:]
Frau Dr. Jeanne Lampl-de Groot
Berlin-Dahlem, Schumacherplatz 2

95 I.e., crazy; the first Yiddish word in this correspondence.
96 Suzanne Cassirer-Bernfeld was Siegfried Bernfeld's third wife. Together they wrote Bernfeld, S. & Cassirer-Bernfeld, S. (1944). "Freud's Early Childhood." *Bulletin of the Menninger Clinic*, VIII, 107–115.

55.
PROF. DR. FREUD, VIENNA IX., BERGGASSE 19
January 25, 1933

Dear Jeanne,
I hasten to correct a small misunderstanding. The situation with my monies in Berlin is as follows: Paret-C., who has money only in Berlin, will pay Ernst (the first installment at the beginning of February), and Ernst will then defray all expenses from my account. Because the large Goethe Prize he managed has shrunk to about 74 marks, I wrote to him last week that *in the meantime* he may "draw" as he wishes on the credit I have with you (e.g., for Ernstl). But from February on there will be no reason to raid your account, and under no circumstances may he take out so much that none remains for an ample supply of cigars.

Whenever you have it together for an episode of analysis, want to do it, and can justify it, I have time for you, i.e., I will take time away from the others who are not progressing. Ruth is still here, I could not call in the poetess, and despite her attached parasite, S.P.-C. is doing an excellent analysis. She and B. Appear to be very much in love with each other.

My mouth is now almost completely healed – only my immortal nasal catarrh, etc., disturbs function and causes problems. I go to see Pichler once a week. The weather is horrid and mercilessly cold.

I appreciated the good news about yourself as well as your splendid description of Hans's not unfavorable state. I await Eitingon at the end of this week. Once again, Anna was terrifically successful with a lecture in the Psychopath. [!][97] Association, but she really looks as if she is working too hard.

Warm greetings for you and your whole family. I hope that nothing bad is going on with the children.
Your Freud

[Addressed to:]
Frau Dr. Jeanne Lampl-de Groot
Berlin-Dahlem, Schumacherplatz 2

56.
PROF. DR. FREUD, VIENNA IX., BERGGASSE 19
February 1, 1933

My dear Jeanne,
The keenest sympathy from me and us with regard to your domestic epidemic! It cannot have been a good time, but according to the dates in

---

97 Gerhard Fichtner penciled in the exclamation mark because of Freud's slip – or joke: psychopath. Vereinigung instead of psychoan. Vereinigung.

your letters it was only brief, and everything has passed, except for the unwanted relapses of whooping cough in the children. I now wish to detail for you what is happening here so that you won't miss being in Vienna.

The weather has suddenly turned warm. Grippe is everywhere, but not severe anywhere. Ruth is still in bed with pulmonary nodules, but it doesn't seem to be anything worrying. Earlier, Mark was sent to the Cottage Sanatorium with a terrible cold. Marianne Kris thought she was healthy, but then had to deal with a high fever at night. Above us, Bob, Miky, and their American guest are in bed. I just heard that a meeting of the board scheduled for tomorrow was canceled because Deutsch[98] is sick. This meeting was to elect the board of the training institutions because Deutsch resigned, demoralized by the continued attacks from Federn,[99] and Anna declared her solidarity with her. (Federn really appears to be developing into a *grandpère terrible*.) So these are the cases in our closest circle. All of us are still standing, but for how long? I have been discharged by Pichler for the moment, i.e., I have an appointment for February 28, but a florid nasal infection with tubal catarrh which disturbs all functions because of swelling has prevented me from enjoying this rare time off. Eitingon did not look well; however, we found him more sociable and talkative than usual. Bullitt appeared again like a meteor. We hope that he will soon have an influential position; he is on very intimate terms with Roosevelt. But nothing is certain. He thinks that as long as Neurath retains the Foreign Ministry, the internal affairs are of little importance. We are all waiting expectantly to see what becomes of Reich Chancellor Hitler's program, whose only concrete point is Jew-baiting. – Bernfeld appears to continue acting stupidly in his private life; Frau P. is very interesting, her character picture still wavering.

I hope for your recovery and – a lovely healthy time for a change.

Warmly, Your Freud

[Addressed to:]
Frau Dr. Jeanne Lampl-de Groot
Berlin-Dahlem, Schumacherplatz 2

98 Helene Deutsch (née Rosenbach; 1884–1982) was one of the first women to study medicine in Vienna. She did her psychiatric training in Wagner-Jauregg's clinic, where Jeanne also received her training. She then started her training analysis with Freud and continued it in 1923 with Karl Abraham. In 1922 she founded the Vienna Psychoanalytical Institute and became its first director; Bernfeld was the vice director and Anna Freud the secretary. Deutsch emigrated to the United States in 1935. She published works on the psychology of women, on psychoanalytic technique, and on psychiatric syndromes such as the "as-if personality."

99 Paul Federn (1871–1950) was a Viennese physician and psychoanalyst. From 1924 to 1938 he was "acting head of the Vienna Psychoanalytical Society" (Fichtner, G. [2004]. "für den sein Elend geniessenden Dulder" [for the Patient Sufferer Enjoying His Misery]. In *Jahrbuch Psychoanalyse*, 49, 170–175).

57.
PROF. DR. FREUD, VIENNA IX., BERGGASSE 19
February 10, 1933

Dear Jeanne,
You succeeded admirably in your realistic portrayal of the post-grippe misery in your house. It can't have been pleasant. The characteristic of this pestilence, that one recovers only slowly from it, has proven to be the case here as well. Marianne, Ruth, and Deutsch are on their feet again. But now Anna is a patient, but with a low temperature and few symptoms, perhaps protected by the quinine she took beforehand, but she is isolated from the others. I'm getting by with my own old catarrhs.

My conversation with Einstein ("Why War?")[100] has been fully corrected and can be published in February. It won't help humanity either. Why is Einstein doing such foolish things, for example with his profession of faith and other superfluities? Perhaps because he is so good-natured and unworldly.[101] I have had no recent news from Bullitt. I thought he was fantasizing when he complained about persecution from his enemies, but his denunciation in the American Senate proves that he was right, not me. I'm sure you've read about it.[102]

Things are going peculiarly with Paret. The whole world screams that she is unreliable, lies, and fantasizes, and I can't find it. I have to believe her, but don't yet know whether I should in everything. But I do have a firm assessment of Bernfeld because he visited me once, and I can compare his behavior then with his present comportment and his speeches, which I learn about from P. (who is in love with him). It is not favorable to him, as he talks and acts as if in psychosis, confused, contradictory, and completely false toward me. P. claims that he is now finally coming

---

100 The correspondence with Albert Einstein known as "Why War?" was not Freud's idea, but a request from the Arts and Letters subcommittee of the League of Nations International Institute of Intellectual Cooperation, which sought to publicize correspondences of outstanding intellectuals in order to prompt discussion of the League's efforts and goals. Einstein was the first to be invited to contribute, and he suggested Freud as his collocutor. The title was a reference to World War I, which had been the reason for the League's founding, but it also touched on the threat of renewed warfare. Einstein was of the opinion that the churches had a special role to play in preventing war, but Freud pointed to their history of censorship and the horrors of the Holy Inquisition. See Freud, S. (1932). "Why War?" In *Standard Edition*, vol. XXII. London: Hogarth, pp. 197–215.

101 Among other things, in his response to Einstein, Freud described his theory of the death instinct.

102 Bullitt had been present at the 1919 Treaty of Versailles and had opposed many of the most onerous provisions of that treaty. In late January 1933 he was accused by Republican Senator Arthur Robinson, of Indiana, of negotiating with foreign powers over war debts – without being an authorized spokesman of President-elect Roosevelt, and was threatened with prosecution under the Logan Act.

to his senses and admits to his distortions. Not a word of his about this or that analysis merits credence. He describes Lisel[103] to his new lover as a cognac swiller, morphine addict, and pervert. I would entertain that these might be P.'s inventions, but I can count against it what B. says that I told him – which he has since retracted. One of the two, B. or P., is a God-forsaken fool and fantasist, and I think it's our B. Well, it'll become clear.

Warm wishes for a complete recovery!

Your Freud

[Addressed to:]
Frau Dr. Jeanne Lampl-de Groot
Berlin-Dahlem, Schumacherplatz 2

58.
PROF. DR. FREUD, VIENNA IX., BERGGASSE 19
February 16, 1933

My dear Jeanne,

Oh my, what a horrific letter! Matters are really coming to a head right now for you, but certainly not everything is as bad as it looks. The children will soon be healthy, and you too, if you have contracted whooping cough, which isn't impossible. Nor does the tumor impress me, but the other sounds unfavorable and challenges patience and hopefulness. Please excuse the stupid thought, but wouldn't it be a pathogenetically desirable, though banal, solution if Hans's relapse weren't concomitant with your own menopause but with the menstrual disorder of that nice girl?[104] Anything would be better than an endogenous process.[105]

I cannot show you my sympathy better than that I am writing you so quickly, an ersatz for the fact that I would like to speak with you.

Anna has recovered after a relatively short but empty misery.

February 17: The house has remained relatively spared; I devoured quinine prophylactically, otherwise everything seems to be subsiding. Bullitt visited for two days; since then I've heard nothing from him, so no decision has yet been made. As we know from the assassination [attempt],

---

103 Liesl (Elisabeth) Neumann, Bernfeld's second wife, was an actress and cabarettist, later a Hollywood actress.
104 It is in passages like this that we especially miss Jeanne's destroyed letters to Freud. Jeanne was only 37, so menopause would have been unlikely. If she had a menstrual disorder, on the other hand, the "nice girl" whom Freud refers to might have been her.
105 I.e., generated from one's own internal psychic structures, in contrast to *exogenous*, in response to external causes.

Roosevelt was traveling.[106] I'm very anxious because the outcome of the analysis depends partly on that, but also perhaps a bit of the destiny of Europe, because Bullitt is the only American with an understanding of Europe who wants to do something for Europe. This is why I dare not hope that he will actually be given a position in which he can act according to his lights.

I agree with your comparison between men and women as far as unpleasantness is concerned. One can only despise the one sex if one forgets about the other. The Paret files are by no means closed, but one thing is clear, that her being is of a higher order than that of the persons whom she currently runs into at our home. Slanderous exaggerations, such as those she currently makes against Lisel, are really not like her. That can only be traced back to Bernfeld himself. Despite all of her probable defects, she has none of his degeneracy. We will see.

Please write soon. You won't have many other "outlets" given your current tensions.

With warm wishes,
Your Freud

[Addressed to:]
Frau Dr. Jeanne Lampl-de Groot
Berlin-Dahlem, Schumacherplatz 2

59.
PROF. DR. FREUD, VIENNA IX., BERGGASSE 19
February 25, 1933

Dear Jeanne,
The unwelcome call did not come yesterday. We were prepared to answer, first, that you should not come along, and second that I am free at any time to see him, except on Sunday (and this time on Tuesday as well, as I am at Pichler's). For Sunday we would have a visit scheduled (let's say, Arnold Zweig from Berlin). The real reason would of course have been that after his consultation with me, he would have hung around all day with Anna, which would have been of no benefit to him and a terrible burden on her. She thinks it would have been impossible for her to avoid him by retreating to Hochrotherd. Well, it's better this way.

I also know that the conditions that occur under stubborn sleeplessness do not manifest favorably. But one cannot claim it is a symptom of the grippe, which he probably did not avoid. The lack of a doctor is terrible.

---

106 President Roosevelt had just delivered a speech in Miami, Florida, on February 15, 1933, when an unemployed bricklayer fired shots at him, all of which missed.

I mean, one ought to overcome one's prejudice against Simmel[107] and get him involved. I can't see that there's anyone else in Berlin.

Bernfeld has now modified his accusations against Liesel[108] to the extent that very little remains of them. Paret, on the other hand, increasingly gains my trust.

In expectation of news from you, with warm wishes,

Your Freud

[Addressed to:]
Frau Dr. Jeanne Lampl-de Groot
Berlin-Dahlem, Schumacherplatz 2

60.
PROF. DR. FREUD, VIENNA IX., BERGGASSE 19
March 9, 1933

My dear Jeanne,

Yes, you are very harried. I understand everything that you have acceded to against your better judgment, and I know that your behavior would be different if he had developed a severe physical ailment. Unfortunately, a psychic illness removes the ideal character of the person. I don't see what else you could do than to urge him to be treated medically. I cannot judge from a distance the extent to which you may have recourse to threats. The moment and the situation must prompt you. But you see what an unfavorable influence even this minor interference on my part has had. Imagine that he were with me in analysis; a severe outbreak would be unavoidable. I must remain distant from him.

---

107 During the 5th International Congress in Budapest (September 28–29 1918) Ernst Simmel (1881–1947), along with Sándor Ferenczi and Karl Abraham, presented their findings regarding the psychoanalytic treatment of war neuroses. After Abraham's death in 1925, Simmel became the head of the German Psychoanalytical Association, and in the same year founded his (psychoanalytical) sanatorium in Schloss Tegel, outside of Berlin, for the study and treatment of severe cases of neurosis and psychosis. It was closed in 1931 as a consequence of the Great Depression. The "prejudice against Simmel" presumably related to Abraham's remark that Simmel in no way went beyond the perspective of Breuer and Freud, and that he himself had powerful resistance to sexuality of which he was still unaware. Simmel had undergone training analysis with Abraham (Roudinesco, E. & Plon, M. [2004]. *Wörterbuch der Psychoanalyse. Namen, Länder, Werke, Begriffe.* Vienna: Springer, p. 947). On April 12, 1933, Freud wrote that his son Ernst had had problems at the border, and that since that day no German Jew had been permitted to leave the country. He added that Simmel had succeeded in reaching Zurich after a brief arrest by the Gestapo. In a letter from 1938, Simmel reported to Freud on the founding of the Sigmund Freud Clinic in Los Angeles (Jones, E., [1957]. Op. cit., vol. 3, pp. 178, 233).
108 Freud varied the spelling of her name.

And even in other respects, there is nothing to be done other than wait and be glad when one more day has passed without terrifying news. Something very ominous is happening with our small country of Austria; of course, we don't know what. I haven't heard a word from Bullitt; in all probability another false hope has gone by the wayside. The naming of ambassadors has not been made public yet. Pichler is finally working on the prosthesis again instead of on me, which is appreciably less painful. I greet you warmly in all expectation,

   Your Freud

[Addressed to:]
Frau Dr. Jeanne Lampl-de Groot
<u>Berlin-Dahlem</u>, Schumacherplatz 2

61.
[Postcard to both:]
Vienna, March 15, 1933

   Who is the person on two of the three pictures that Edith is holding?
   Warmly, the old, deaf xx[109]

[Addressed to:]
Herr and Frau
Dr. Hans Lampl
<u>Berlin-Dahlem</u>, Schumacherplatz 2

62.
PROF. DR. FREUD, VIENNA IX., BERGGASSE 19
April 8, 1933

   Dear Jeanne,
   I could report even more if I postponed this letter, but your greetings from Nordwijk just arrived, and I have time to write you, when otherwise I would be working because Jackson is already on Easter holiday. Oli and Henny are due to arrive this evening to discuss their future, and tomorrow,

---

109 Freud wrote: "Herzlich der alte, taube xx." This is the only signature of its kind in the correspondence. The postcard was sent shortly after the Reichstag Fire Decree, which nullified many civil liberties in Germany, including privacy of the mail, and made it easier to imprison opponents of the Nazis. Given the ongoing attacks on Jews and their property, Freud may have wanted to screen his name. It has also been suggested that Freud may have intended a hidden meaning: Return home to your mother in Holland. As the signature suggests, Freud was in fact going deaf.

Sunday, I'm to speak with Dr. Paret, who brings news from Ernst. He is now an active Nazi, called here by his wife, from whom he is separated.

All of the questions that you posed to yourself and me I have already considered on my own, and I have come to the conclusion that nothing can be decided in the present state of unclarity. I think that you should return to Berlin in any case because, as a non-German, nothing threatens you, and you have to look after your property. What happens next depends on whether the Institute is closed and analysis banned, and how Hans tolerates these times, pregnant with calamity that does none of us any good. And what then? If this Hitler nonsense continues, and since you have cast your lot with the Jews, then you and your children certainly shouldn't remain in Germany. Thank goodness, and thanks to your old father, you may move freely. You have to see where you can pitch your tent and find work.

But on two points we remain firm, the decision not to move, and the expectation that things cannot become remotely what they are in Germany. We are on a path toward dictatorship by right-wing parties that will ally themselves with the Nazis. All of it less than lovely, but laws of exception against minorities are expressly forbidden in Austria by the peace treaty. The victorious nations will surely not permit the annexation to Germany, and our mob is somewhat less brutal than the Germans to whom they are related. So, we have rented Hohe Warte 46 as of May, where we confidently await you. If not for your justifiable concerns about how Hans will respond to Vienna, Vienna as a solution for you would be obvious.

Physically I am not doing badly. Pichler is finally working on the prosthesis instead of on my tissue. My new ones are interesting and satisfactory; we sent Ernstl with Bob, Mabbie, and a teacher to Sicily over Easter; he, too, is a serious problem! JoFi had a dangerous birth, but is now well, and proud of her two little rat-like offspring. We will have to sacrifice something for Abraham's family; Ophuijsen is very brave and diligent. Warm greetings for you and hopefully news from you soon.

Your Freud

[Addressed to:]
Frau Dr Jeanne Lampl de Groot
The Hague, Holland, Belvedereweg 11

63.
PROF. DR. FREUD, VIENNA IX., BERGGASSE 19
April 15, 1933

My dear Jeanne,
Today is my first day of vacation, and besides that, the last day of a 47-year medical practice. Let us take the opportunity, which will soon come to an end once you have returned to Berlin, to talk freely.

a) It is interesting that our paranoid cases move in the direction of improvement at the same time. Not only that your Hans is, thankfully, doing so well; Federn, who definitely has something similar, also behaves more calmly, and even Ferenczi, whose delusions have become terribly pronounced (accompanied by the most serious physical symptoms of regression), is returning to levelheadedness, writes friendly letters and is following the advice to stop work for several weeks. Perhaps he's only dissimulating. I know too little about Harník.[110]

b) Dr. Paret did not wish to visit me. He's not a Jew, but the son of a pastor; additionally, judging from afar, he's a constitutional psychopath with insanity the probable outcome. Strangely, Bernfeld, who has spoken with him, views him quite similarly. I know his wife much better. She is refined, very talented, thoroughly distinguished, but terribly scattered, and despite all efforts, quite helpless. Her relationship with Bernfeld is not going well; he's not at her level, an unorderly person. That I would take him in analysis is impossible because of Paret, but also for my own sake.

c) The impression I got from Oli's visit was depressing. He comports himself well, doesn't whine, looks for work, and is prepared to work hard. But nonetheless his prospects are terrible. He vacillates between Spain and Palestine, but has no supports in either place. Nor does she seem especially suited as an emigree or pioneer. (That is to say, Henny.) They returned to Berlin yesterday for the purpose of leaving the house for good. Ernst has postponed his visit to early May.

d) Simmel is in Zurich; I don't think that Mrs. Abraham is there, however. I know that Jones is working with Ophuijsen on aid for the A. family. We should contribute.

e) "Warum Krieg?" [Why War?] is available from the publisher; however, it is not being sold in G., although it has already appeared in French and English.[111]

f) Ruth has been sick forever, coughs, has a fever, was unable to attend analysis. Marianne has discontinued ever since the new patient was admitted. My English poetess is very interesting, as is my Dutchman, van der Leeuw,[112] the brother of Ruth's patient, people from Rotterdam. Neither of them for very long.

---

110 Jenö Harnik was a Hungarian psychoanalyst.
111 The correspondence was also published in Dutch. See Einstein, A. & Freud, S. (1933). *Waarom Oorlog?* Ed. Institut International de Coöperation Intellectuelle. Amsterdam: Uitgeversbedrijf N.V. Seyffardt's Boek- en Muziekhandel.
112 Dr. J. J. (Koos) van der Leeuw (1893–1934) was in analysis with Freud. His brother, Dr. C. H. (Cees) van der Leeuw (1890–1973), was in analysis with Ruth Mack Brunswick. They built the Van Nelle Factory, a modernistic industrial building designed by the architectural firm of Brinkman & van der Vlugt. The building has recently been recognized as a UNESCO World Cultural Heritage Site. Freud called Koos van der Leeuw "the flying Dutchman." Both brothers died in airplane accidents.

g) Robert has a bad case of the grippe; Mathilde appears to have been infected as well. Mark is embarking for New York today; his father is deathly ill. Isn't that news enough? Enjoy your few days in Holland!

Warmly, Your Freud

[Address:]
Frau Dr. Jeanne Lampl de Groot
The Hague, Holland, Belvedereweg 11

64.
PROF. DR. FREUD, VIENNA IX., BERGGASSE 19
May 26, 1933

My dear Jeanne,

It was exactly as you described in your letter. A feeling of confusion, and of relief that he[113] has now escaped this terrible decay. Over the past few weeks he could barely stand or walk, and the delusion was much worse than we had known. But there is also the pain at our loss, especially because of what he had meant to us, although he had been dead to us for years. But the final, brutal fact has a particular power.

Anna and Martin attended the funeral from our house; Federn, Frau Deutsch, and perhaps a few others were there as well. Anna returned completely shaken. The woman was completely lucid, resigned, and genuinely unhappy. He apparently died suddenly from a quite unexpected respiratory arrest.

Jones was very friendly from a distance. – One more dark shadow in these dark times. I learned from Meng,[114] who was here yesterday, that Landauer[115] will be allowed to remain in Stockholm. *De Groene*

---

113 I.e., Sándor Ferenczi.
114 Along with Franz Alexander, Heinrich Meng (1887–1972) belonged to the "promising younger generation."
115 Karl Landauer (1887–1945) was born in Munich and came from a Jewish banking family. He trained as a psychoanalyst under Freud before World War I and was a training analyst of Max Horkheimer (1895–1973), among others. In 1926 he was founder of the Southwest German Psychoanalytic Working Group (1920–1933), in Frankfurt, and in 1929 he, together with Meng, Frieda Fromm-Reichmann, and Erich Fromm, founded the Frankfurt Psychoanalytic Institute, which worked closely with the renowned Frankfurt Institute for Social Research. When the Institute was shuttered by the Nazis and the books confiscated, Landauer fled first to Sweden, then in 1933 to Holland, where he worked as a training analyst. However, in 1943 he was captured by the Gestapo in Amsterdam and deported. He died of starvation and exhaustion in Bergen-Belsen in 1945, shortly before the liberation of the camp. (See Landauer, K. (1991). *Theorie der Affekte und andere Schriften zur Ich-Organisation*. Frankfurt: Fischer Taschenbuch Verlag). The gripping correspondence (1934–1941) between Landauer in the Netherlands and

Amsterdammer[116] has published a translation of "Warum Krieg?" over two issues. We thank you for the news of Lux's[117] recovery and our children's travel plans. Ruth and Mark returned day before yesterday; the Princess is said to have real plans.

Warm greetings to all,

Freud

[Address:]

Frau Dr. Jeanne Lampl-de Groot

Berlin-Dahlem, Schumacherplatz 2

65.

PROF. DR. FREUD, VIENNA IX., BERGGASSE 19

June 8, 1933

My dear Jeanne,

The memorial for Ferenczi took up all of Pentecost; it was in no way an easy matter. Now all I feel in its wake is emptiness.

Other than that, little has happened, an interesting visit from H.G. Wells,[118] too little news from the children in London and Paris.

My mouth continues to hurt terribly. Fo and Tattoun[119] are cute and very naughty; I'm worried about where they will be placed in the fall. All plans that we hear about seem to be built on sand; nowhere is the outside world hospitable. There is no sign of a cultural conscience; everyone is bent on immediate profit.

I spoke briefly with Sachs.[120] Unfavorable impression; the vulgarity that he had always displayed was all the more on display. Like a nouveau riche, fat, self-satisfied, smug, snobbish, charmed by America, and full of

---

Horkheimer, who had by then fled to the United States, is contained in Horkheimer, M. (1995). *Gesammelte Schriften*, vols. 15–17. Frankfurt: S. Fischer Verlag. On May 4, 2010, Lex Janssen, president of the Dutch Psychoanalytical Society, unveiled a memorial to Landauer and August Watermann, who was also an analyst and victim of Jewish persecution in Holland.

116 Einstein's letter is on pages 1 and 2 of *De Groene Amsterdammer*, No. 2914, April 8, 1933. Freud's letter is printed on pages 1 to 3 of No. 2915, April 15, 1933. It was banned in Germany.

117 Lux (also called Lucie or Lucia) Brasch married Freud's youngest son Ernst on May 18, 1920. She had already emigrated to London with their three sons; Ernst joined them somewhat later after selling his office and house in Berlin.

118 Herbert George Wells (1866–1946) was an author, pioneer in science fiction (*War of the Worlds, The Time Machine*), historian, and sociologist. He visited Freud several times.

119 JoFi's puppies. Tattoun was later adopted by the Lampl-de Groot family; however, he had to be left behind in Vienna when they fled to Holland in 1938, much to the children's disappointment (Edith Berkovits-Lampl, 2011).

120 Hanns Sachs had since settled in Boston.

his great successes there. Anna was right to raise the question of what one should wish for such people. Misfortune doesn't do them any good, and they can't tolerate success.

You may have noticed that I'm in a bad mood.

Warmly, your Freud

[Address:]
Frau Dr. Jeanne Lampl de Groot
<u>Berlin-Dahlem</u>, Schumacherplatz 2

66.
PROF. DR. FREUD, VIENNA IX., BERGGASSE 19
July 14, 1933

My dear Jeanne,

What a relief to be able to write to you at a different address. You, too, must experience this change as a pleasure. And then, of course, there is the unique beauty of Lake Carezza. Somehow I recall a narrow path between thick beds of moss as something special.

What you write about Sachs comports completely with my impression. The vulgarity that always exhibited has now come to predominate. With a layer of snobbism now plastered on top. Radó, surely as *meshugge* as you describe him, is certainly the warmer and more reliable. Harnik, as I am sure you know, is already in Budapest, at an institute.

Very little pleasant to report about us. The summer is bad, the house itself is very hot when the weather is. (I interrupt to switch to what I just heard from Martin, that Sachs has donated £300 to the Verlag. This is to be counted in his favor.) Too many illnesses, in part not yet run their course. Ruth is still in a sanatorium after a cervical operation (thankfully benign). Ernstl had a tonsillectomy; after a week of secondary bleeding, now finally healed and discharged. Martin is fighting a tedious furunculosis and spent several days in bed; Anna has suffered greatly from a tooth extraction; still has bone pain and a temperature. She is so worn down that I insist that she take August off from all her obligations, either travel or seclude herself in HRE,[121] where she will be unreachable for all. I myself hope not to hold any sessions in August, unless the Princess visits me for a time. Unfortunately, I won't have anything else to fill my time this year; I wouldn't know what to write and wouldn't be in the mood anyway.

Fo and Tattoun have developed marvelously, are almost as big as their mother, very boisterous and get into all sorts of mischief. I hope that Sachs's friend Mrs. McPherson will take them in the fall because we can't

---

121 I.e., Hochrotherd.

keep them. Unfortunately, Jofi disturbs our animal idyl, treating poor Lün [JoFi's sister] so badly. An awkward situation!

Politics after the dogs! Quiet, for now. We may assume that we are headed for a particular homegrown fascism that will not be as brutal as the German. Whether it will be pleasant to live in Vienna? I am anxious to hear about your plans.

Warm greetings to all!

Your Freud

[Addressed to:]
Frau Dr. Jeanne Lampl de Groot
Hotel Carezza al Lago, Dolomites, Italy

67.
PROF. DR. FREUD, VIENNA IX., BERGGASSE 19
July 27, 1933

Dear Jeanne,
The prevalence of illness is improving here, but the news that you intend to increase it is intolerable. There is little medically from your description that would indicate the appendix; I hope that you are careful in this regard.

Ruth is well again, she had tears in her cervix and had surgery. She wants to travel to America in mid-August because her father is very ill. I expect you [to arrive] at about the same time. Except for the risk for Hans, I am very happy about this resolution. It will be very nice to have you here to enlarge our family. There is only one thing to consider, to prevent Hans from leaning on Anna. She was so exhausted that I became worried about her for the first time. I insisted that she withdraw from all work and obligations in August, and I am setting an example for her.

Politically, I had anticipated a right-wing dictatorship under Dollfuss[122] but without the Nazis. It is doubtful whether that will come to pass. And it wouldn't be ideal anyway.

Very nice letters from the three boys on Mama's birthday, and a sad one from Lux. For her, emigration means the most.

Warm greetings (and a little climate envy)

From your Freud

[Addressed to:]
Frau Dr Jeanne Lampl de Groot
Grand Hotel Carezza al Lago, Dolomites, Italy

---

122 Engelbert Dollfuss (1892–1934), the Austrian chancellor and dictator who sought to establish a Catholic-based "Austrofascism" that would be independent of the Nazis. He was assassinated on July 25, 1934, when Austrian Nazis stormed the chancellery.

68.
PROF. DR. FREUD, VIENNA IX., BERGGASSE 19
Grinzing, August 12, 1937

My dear Jeanne,

I'm answering you immediately, which I can do because I'm on complete vacation.

Happy that things are beginning to go well for you. The baths are no empty mania, and it is generally the case that such improvement persists and is successful. You will come to enjoy [Bad] Gastein. That nonsense with P. L. must have been funny.

We are all very well, except that everyone around us is sick. We now have three "aunts" at the Perchtoldsdorf Sanatorium. Ditha Heller's[123] uncanny illness had an unexpectedly salubrious outcome. Anna is enjoying her relative holiday freedom. I had no need to complain, except for localized ailments that change in form, but are always present. A continuation of the Moses essay is finished, again only a portion. The rest will never be written. The garden is more beautiful than ever. Lün is lazy, very lovable, and not yet free of eczema, which mars her beauty.

I see nothing that would bar me from giving you a few sessions that you want when you come again. Your continued analysis will result in heights of completeness that are rarely achieved.

Convey my regards to your mother, about whom you report good news, and convey greetings to the other members of your small but interesting family.

Warmly,

Your Freud

[Addressed to:]
Frau Dr. Jeanne Lampl
Badgastein, Pension Grammer

68a.
[Between the letters there is a sheet of A4 paper with printed letterhead with the new residence and practice address in Amsterdam:
Jeanne Lampl-de Groot
Zenuwarts Tel., 725939
Amsterdam-Z 19
Haringvlietstraat 39

as well as a handwritten note by Jeanne]:
"We lived in Vienna from the end of August 1933 to the end of May 1938."

---

123 Judith Heller (1885–1977), Freud's beloved niece, daughter of his sister Anna Bernays (1858–1955).

69.
PROF. DR. FREUD, 39 ELSWORTHY ROAD, LONDON, N.W.3
June 13, 1938

My dear Jeanne,

So, we have now really arrived in England; it is very lovely, and the public, friends as well as strangers, have prepared a warm reception for us. (The climate is less warm.)

Ernst rented a charming little house for us; my room opens out onto a veranda that is framed by its own garden and field of flowers, and a view onto a large park with trees. Of course it is only temporary for three months. Ernst is still looking for something permanent that must meet specifications that are rarely realized here. It is difficult for us to live vertically instead of horizontally. It would be even nicer if Aunt Minna[124] weren't so seriously ill and in bed on the top floor. For now she seems to be out of danger.

Naturally everything is still unaccustomed and as if unreal, a clear sense of alienation. One misses too much. It was also strange that you weren't here with us last Saturday morning to disturb me in a negotiation with our little antiquarian. Regarding your future, I have formed the certain expectation that your hardened compatriots will eventually soften up and accept you into their fatherland. At the beginning, they also rejected the previous wave of emigrants, and yet all were able to remain. And The Hague is not far from London.

With warm greetings for you, Mother, Hans, and the little Dutch girls,
Your Freud

[Addressed to:]
Frau Dr. Jeanne Lampl-de Groot
Belvedereweg 11, The Hague, Holland

70.
[Postcard from London:]
39 Elsworthy Road, NW 3
July 8, 1938

Quickly, warm well-wishes regarding the good news, which I never doubted. There is not enough for a letter at this time. I'm overwhelmed with responsibilities and writings. But naturally, until we see each other again!

---

124 Minna Bernays (1865–1941) was Freud's sister-in-law. She had lived with the family in the Berggasse.

Warm greetings to all,
Freud

[Addressed to:]
Frau Dr. Jeanne Lampl-de Groot
Belvedereweg 11, ~~The Hague~~, Holland

71.
PROF. DR. FREUD ~~VIENNA, IX., BERGGASSE 19~~.
[London] 39 Elsworthy Rd, NW3
July 26, 1938

Dear Jeanne,
That you write so regularly is a good ersatz for our half hours on Saturday mornings. I would have liked it if you could have reported better things. I am becoming so intolerant of Hans, the way one does of patients who are disobedient. What does the fellow actually want? He's already had everything, diagnosis, prognosis, treatment, everything has been clearly laid out; why doesn't he simply stop? I understand that under the circumstances you don't want to put any additional stress on him.

You will see Anna in Paris; she was able with great effort to obtain a travel permit from the authorities. We expect that the Congress[125] will bring a final separation from the Americans who have become so irritating, and thus create clear relations. This time I am represented in absentia with a lecture.

Things are very lively here, not an hour of boredom. Our possessions haven't arrived yet. Will they ever, or are the thieves contemplating some new extortion?

I am not yet properly supplied with doctors; there is no lack of new circumstances.

Warm greetings,
Your Freud

[Addressed to:]
Frau Dr. Jeanne Lampl-de Groot
~~Belvedereweg 11, The Hague, Holland~~
[forwarded:]
Hôtel Regina de Passy, 6 Rue de la Tour
Paris XVIe, France

---

125 The 15th International Psychoanalytical Congress, which was held in Paris, in August 1938, dealt with the problem of lay analysis (Jones, E. [1957]. Op. cit., pp. 299–301).

72.
PROF. DR. FREUD, VIENNA IX., BERGGASSE 19.
[From London] August 22, 1938

My dear Jeanne,
Finally good news from you! And why not? Life is so colorful, and we have been so richly supplied with the bad lately. I was surprised only by your disclosure that you are seeking a house – in Amsterdam. I remember how little distances mean to you. Perhaps all of Holland is not larger than London? In any event, it has fewer inhabitants than this great city.

But you want to hear from us. So: *20 Maresfield Gardens* will hopefully be our last address on this planet, but not to be used before the end of September. Our own house![126] You can imagine how much of our shrunken assets it cost us. And much too nice for us; not too far from here, and from Ernst, who is transforming the house into a ruin in order to rehabilitate it for our needs. He is building an elevator, making one room out of two, or vice versa, pure "witches one-times-one," in architectural terms. The happy expectation of such a lovely possession is unfortunately clouded by all manner of shadows, Aunt Minna's illness, the gravest of all.

So, rein in your desire to visit us until we are able to present to you the fully constituted palace. In the meantime, we are subject to an uncomfortable provision, namely that we must move out of this house by September 5. We will be forced to spend weeks in a hotel, Aunt in a hospital or so-called sanatorium, all of which are unbelievably unsatisfactory. A country of contrasts, in some respects quite backward.

My mouth is giving me no real peace. In Vienna, I would have been operated on long ago as a precaution. Other things aren't moving forward either; neither Martin nor Robert has found employment. However, it is the deadest part of the season. Ruth is still here (until the 24th) and is taking some follow-up analysis, which will probably do her good. How incomplete my earlier analyses were!

Willi Lévy molded me [in clay], almost finished. Yesterday I sat for a photographer who, to judge by his samples, produces special works of art. If it comes out well, you'll get a picture.

And now warm greetings to all of you! Don't drop all of your Viennese habits.

Your Freud

[Addressed to:]
Frau Dr Jeanne Lampl-de Groot
Belvedereweg 11, <u>The Hague</u>, Holland

---

126 "Eigenes" corrected from the original text "Ein einiges Haus!" which means "A united house!"

73.
PROF. DR. FREUD ~~VIENNA, IX., BERGGASSE 19.~~
20 Maresfield Gardens, NW3
October 8, 1938

My dear Jeanne,

I will answer all of your questions in the order in which they appear in your letter. There are good things to report and bad. But first, many thanks for your detailed and primarily happy news about yourself, husband, children, and the new circumstances.[127]

How am I? Slow recovery from the surgery, which was the worst since 1923, which was also made with an incision from outside. I still can't eat and smoke properly, find it difficult to speak, the pain is receding, I'm working three hours a day again. The next few weeks, when the lip has been innervated again and the prosthesis modified to accommodate the new conditions, will probably bring further improvement.

My own home. It is very nice, which I hope you will soon attest to. Light, comfortable, roomy, the only thing missing is a guestroom, which had to be sacrificed to accommodate the elevator. All of the Egyptians, Chinese, and the Greek women[128] arrived, having survived the transport with only minor damage, and they look even more imposing than they did in the Berggasse. Except for one thing: a collection to which nothing is added is actually dead. Our good little Wadler,[129] whom you used to meet in my home on Saturday mornings – he has since poisoned himself with gas.

Aunt Minna, a sad chapter. Still suffering badly from her heart, and now tortured by cystitis, cared for by two nurses who make my wife unhappy because they occupy the living room and bathroom on the first floor. A housewife could be very satisfied in a lovely new house, if the windows,

---

127 The Lampl-de Groot family had since then moved to Haringvlietstraat 39, in Amsterdam, where Jeanne and Hans lived with their two children and had their practices. Jeanne continued to live there until her death.

128 Some of the small sculptures in Freud's collection were ancient.

129 Robert Wadler (1906–1938) was a Jewish archaeologist who advised Freud about what to select from his sculpture collection before his forced emigration. On May 14 Freud noted in a letter to Minna Bernays, who at the time was in a sanatorium in Switzerland, "Herr Wadler will look after our packed belongings after our departure." And on May 23 he wrote, "I'm now waiting to hear from a bookseller whom Wadler recommended [Paul Sonnenfeld], who will take the books that we leave behind." Wadler committed suicide on September 4, probably because he saw no way out of the persecution of Jews that had begun in Vienna. The death report in the Vienna City Archive dated September 8, 1938, gives the cause of death as "Suicide by gas" (Fichtner, G. [2008]. "ein Stück kleines Emigrantenelend neben dem großen." A 1938 Letter from Freud to Jeanne Lampl-de Groot. In C. Frank, L. Hermann & H. Hinz (eds.), *Jahrbuch der Psychoanalyse*, vol. 57. Stuttgart: Frommann-Holzboog, fn. 9, pp. 201–213, 209).

doors, central heating, and lighting didn't constantly necessitate workers, who are very hard to get. In short, it is a small piece of emigrant misery beside the large. With all its wondrous notes, England is a country for the rich and healthy. Nor should one be too old.

Anna is being courageous and is already very busy. Martin is sick again, returned quite worn down from the hospital. These are a few glimpses into our current circumstances.

I have no doubt that you will gain work and influence in Holland. Actually, only in Vienna did we conduct proper analyses.

It is best not to write about the political situation. There were a few bad days with the trenches[130] in the parks and sending the children away,[131] etc.

With warm greetings to all of you,
Your Freud

[Addressed to:]
Frau Dr Jeanne Lampl-de Groot
Haringvlietstraat 39, <u>Amsterdam</u>, Holland

74.
PROF. SIGM. FREUD, 20 MARESFIELD GARDENS
LONDON, N.W. 3
TEL: HAMPSTEAD 2002
November 20, 1938

My dear Jeanne,
Your letter of the 14th of this month is as endearing and reasonable as all the previous ones, but to my joy richer in good news. Among the best is that you are getting into a position in your new-old fatherland where you can make use of your analytic superiority, which is undoubted. I also see no reason why you in particular should be thinking of emigrating. I hope that you will feel ever more contented in Holland, and it will take a long time before the Nazis occupy that country – if it happens at all.

The same elements that create the atmosphere where you are, make themselves felt here as well. The news from ††† Germany,[132] the waves of emigration that beat down on these shores, the insecurity that a near future can bring, all these preclude a real sense of contentment. Apart from that, if one can overlook what is happening, some things are lovely

---

130 I.e., air-raid trenches.
131 The planned evacuation of children and invalids (Fichtner, G. [2008]. Op. cit., pp. 201–213, 211).
132 Freud sometimes used three daggers to indicate that something was tricky, devilish, or an evil to be averted.

here. Especially the house, which you will like when you and Hans visit us for the first time. We are living with and amid all of our own things. I don't think that you will have to forgo yours yet.[133] Aunt Minna is mobile again. Yesterday she came down to the dining room for the first time. The nice little elevator that Ernst had installed has nullified the difference between up and down, and the two prisoners who are unable to navigate the stairs have regained their freedom. Anna is very busy, though mostly with her old cases. No new ones have erred their way to me either. In this respect London is a disappointment. In Anna's opinion, the group here is impossible, and although she takes part in meetings, etc., she has decided to withdraw rather than get into hopeless polemics. Nor has anyone asked me what I think of Melanie Klein's[134] renowned school.

Martin will probably turn up in Holland soon, because he has business with our publisher there. Little Ernst has had the greatest success here thus far; he has become self-sustaining as a result of an exhibition in a large photographic gallery. Mathilde's business also looks promising.

My damned bone spur still hasn't come loose; my symptoms remain unchanged.

Warm greetings to you all,
Your Freud

[Addressed to:]
Dr. Jeanne Lampl de Groot
<u>Amsterdam-Z</u>, Haringvlietstraat 39

75.
PROF. SIGM. FREUD[135]
20 MARESFIELD GARDENS. LONDON, N.W. 3.
TEL: HAMPSTEAD 2002
December 29, 1938

Dear Doctor,
I am writing you immediately after my letter to the Society of Friends, which Augenfeld dictated. Hopefully it will be successful. I answered

---

133 In fact, all of the Lampls' possessions were later confiscated.
134 Melanie Klein (1882–1960) was a prominent psychoanalyst. Her conception of child development, especially of the early stage, are important additions to the theory and technique of child analysis. They gave rise to years of dispute among the various schools (King, P. & Steiner, R. [eds.]. (1991). *The Freud-Klein Controversies 1941–45*. London/New York: Routledge.
135 Letters 75 and 76 were the two letters that were restricted until 2008. Neither was of particular interest. This letter was written to Hans Lampl alone.

your inquiry regarding Selecta,[136] noting that the quality and draw are acceptable, but that I would prefer a shorter and thicker type. With warm New Year's wishes for you, Jeanne, and the children,

Your faithful Freud

[Addressed to:]
Herr Dr. Hans Lampl
<u>Amsterdam-Z</u> Haringvlietstraat 39

76.
PROF. SIGM. FREUD, 20 MARESFIELD GARDENS.
LONDON, N.W. 3
TEL: HAMPSTEAD 2002
[handwritten:] April 3, 1939, To Dr. Hans Lampl and Dr. Jeanne Lampl,
Amsterdam

Dear friends,[137]
I am glad to hear you want to come over to see all of us and am looking forward to your visit at Easter-time.

Yours affectionately, Prof. Freud

[Addressed to:]
Herr and Frau Dr. Hans Lampl
Amsterdam-Z., Holland
Haringvlietstraat 39

Sigmund Freud died on September 23, 1939, with the medical assistance of his physician Max Schur. Although Ernest Jones's listing of mourners included the Lampls,[138] they were in fact not present at the cremation. Separate letters of condolence from Jeanne and Hans addressed to Anna Freud are housed in the Archive of the Dutch Psychoanalytical Association in the De Bazel City Archive, Amsterdam.[139]

---

136 A brand of cigars.
137 Written in English, and not in Sütterlin script.
138 Jones, E. (1957). Op. cit., p. 246.
139 For the text of both letters, see the chapter Jeanne Lampl-de Groot – Biographical Notes.

Figure 23 Jeanne and Hans, The Hague, 1938.

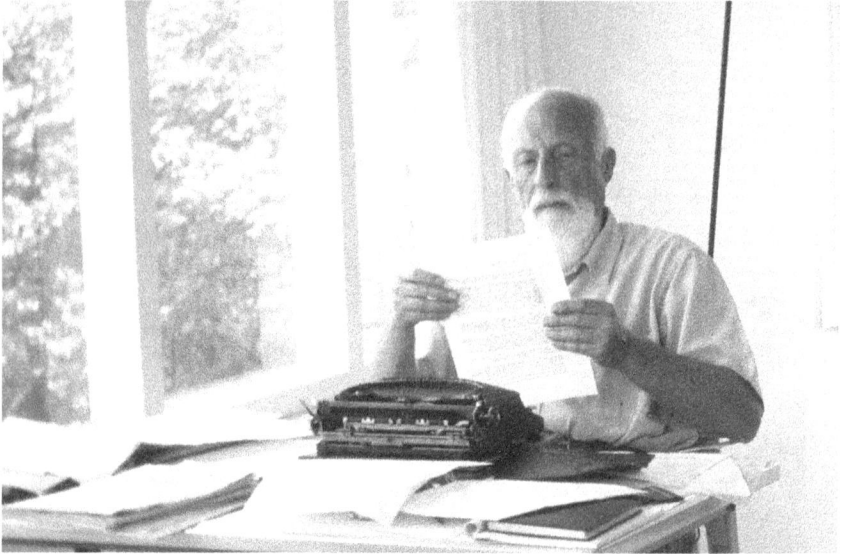

Figure 24 Hans Lampl, Wapenveld, 1957.
Photo: Robert Berkovits

Figure 25 Hans Lampl, ca. 1924.

Figure 26 University of Amsterdam Medical Center, April 1982. Jeanne Lampl-de Groot, to her left Prof. Piet Kuiper, right: Frans de Jonghe, behind: Berthold Gersons, front: Jan Swinkels; all three later became university professors.

Figure 27 IPA Congress, London 1975. From left to right: Jeanne Lampl-de Groot, Leo Rangell, Anna Freud, and Serge Lebovici (Gertie Bögels Archive).

Figure 28 Jeanne and Driek van der Sterren. Münchenwiler, Switzerland, April 1962.

Figure 29 Jeanne and Anna Freud, Schiphol Airport, Amsterdam, ca. 1960.

Figure 30 Jeanne Lampl-de Groot wearing the Freud ring on her right hand, ca. 1950.

Figure 31 Honorary doctorate granted at the University of Amsterdam, 1970; Jeanne's daughter Henriëtte is in the background.

Figure 32 Jeanne Lampl and Heinz Kohut, August 1976.

Figure 33 Jeanne in Wapenveld, November 1980.

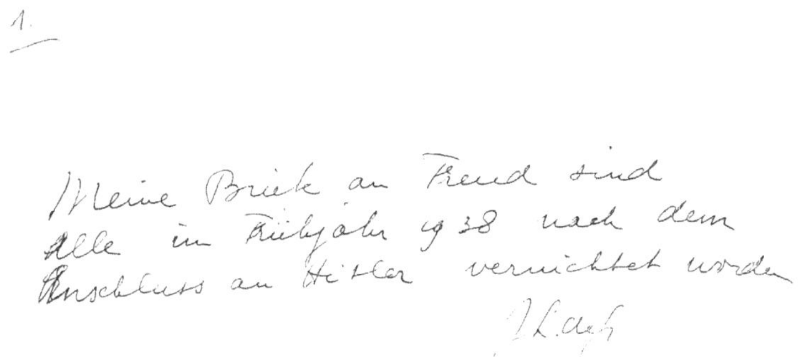
1.

Meine Briefe an Freud sind
alle im Frühjahr 1938 nach dem
Anschluss an Hitler vernichtet worden

Figure 34 Jeanne's note found among Freud's letters stating that her letters to Freud had been destroyed in the spring of 1938, after the Annexation. (Library of Congress).

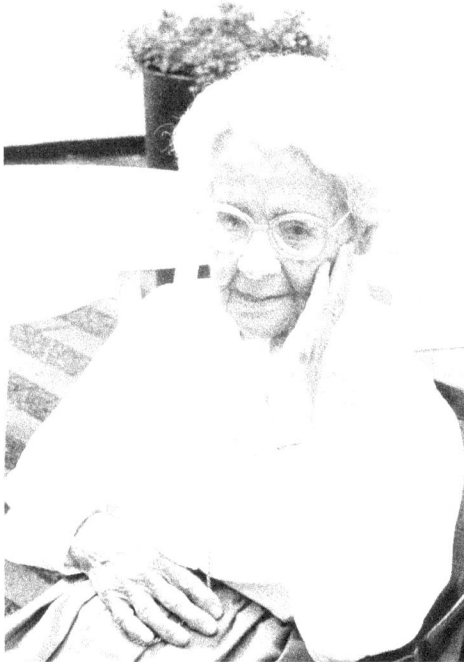

Figure 35 Jeanne at the IPA Congress, Hamburg, July 1985.

Photo: Judy Weinshel, San Francisco

Letter Fragments from Jeanne Lampl-de Groot to her Parents (1921–1923)

Unlike Jeanne Lampl's letters to Freud, the originals of her correspondence with her parents had been preserved, as I discovered in 2009 on one of my visits to Edith und Robert Berkovits-Lampl. Jeanne numbered her letters and numerous picture postcards, sometimes using Arabic and sometimes Roman numerals. Parts of this correspondence have been included in this volume because of the light they shed on her personal development and on her relationship with Freud. They consist of two parts. The first part comprises the letters from Jeanne's five-month trip to Italy from September 28, 1921, to February 13, 1922. The letters begin in Milan after Jeanne had parted with her parents, who returned to The Hague by way of Switzerland and Germany. Her letters are a detailed, almost weekly, travelogue of her impressions of Italy, the Italians, the cities that she and her travel companion T. explored, and the museums that they visited. She also wrote about her plans to visit Vienna, and about the first two letters she received from Freud, as well as his response to her request to undergo psychoanalysis with him, along with her reactions.

The second part, from April 18, 1922, to April 30, 1923, comprises reports on her year in Vienna. In them she discussed her initial worries about lodgings, her bewilderment at the fast pace of life in post-war Vienna, where the scars of World War I were still evident, and the waves of anti-Semitism that flared up regularly.

Jeanne also described her first psychoanalytic sessions with Freud in the Berggasse and her impressions of him. She kept her parents, especially her mother, informed of events, her analysis, and her surroundings. She described her colleagues, especially Freud's daughter Anna. Opera and concert performances were important to her, and she even managed to rent a piano for her room, where she practiced with other amateur musicians. There are also fascinating passages in which she tried to "educate" her mother about the theory and practice of psychoanalysis.

Already in her letters from Italy, Jeanne, more or less at her mother's suggestion, began to consider analyzing her acquaintance H., who at the time was in analysis with van Ophuijsen but was clearly not getting much benefit from it. Jeanne also recommended reading material to her mother,

DOI: 10.4324/9781003268130-4

about which they had a lively back-and-forth. She had briefer written "conversations" with her father, in which, among other things, she complained that he didn't write often enough. In particular, she made clear to him how expensive life was in Vienna. It was also very cold, and she needed more money for warm clothes. He was somewhat suspicious of psychoanalysis and expressed his concerns that Freud might be keeping her in analysis for financial reasons. Jeanne mounted a reasoned and convincing defense of Freud and of herself: Freud, she wrote, could treat much wealthier Americans if he wanted to; however, he considered Jeanne to be extraordinarily well-suited for this profession. As the Austrian crown continued to lose value, she asked her father for donations for her Viennese acquaintances and for the Psychoanalytischer Verlag. Payment to Freud was sometimes made in cigars, a more stable currency. Apparently at Freud's behest, she often got him to transfer money for her analysis, in Dutch guilders, to Ernest Jones in London.

One notable detail in this regard is Freud's apparent suggestion that money – in guilders – be donated to one of his impoverished former Russian patients who had once been a wealthy man but had been impoverished in the wake of the Russian Revolution. This Russian can only have been Sergei Pankejeff, who became famous as the Wolf-Man. He was one of the patients whom Freud treated without asking for remuneration. Muriel Gardiner wrote in detail about this analysis, and Pankejeff's subsequent one with Ruth Mack Brunswick, a later friend of Jeanne's.[1]

She also asked for money for her Italian travel companion, who was planning to get married. From her brief thank-yous, we may assume that he complied more or less willingly. At one point, she asked him to become more involved in financial questions, for which she had up to then felt little responsibility.

From the letters, it is clear that Jeanne quickly felt at home in the Viennese psychoanalytic world. She got to know her lecturers, enjoyed the courses, made friends, and accompanied them to the mountains over the weekends. The shyness that she had always felt seemed to have disappeared.

These letters to her parents came to an end in 1923, at a time when she was beginning to blossom in every respect. I selected the letter fragments primarily with regard to how they illuminate the development of psychoanalysis as a scientific discipline, treatment techniques, international organizations, and professional training methods. I selected passages that describe the atmosphere and circumstances in which these developments

---

1 Gardiner, M. (ed.). (1971). *The Wolf-Man, by the Wolf-Man: With "The Case of the Wolf-Man"*. New York: Basic Books. The book, with a foreword by Anna Freud and a supplement by Ruth Mack Brunswick, contains analyses of the Wolf-Man by Sigmund Freud and Brunswick. It also contains Brunswick's recollections about his life and treatment, and Gardiner's encounters with him until 1956.

took place, and additionally ones that demonstrate Jeanne's personal contributions to these developments. Fragments in which Jeanne cited or paraphrased Freud are unabridged, and it is remarkable how faithful she was in citing passages that can be verified. Her writing style is matter-of-fact, but not unemotional, and she did not hesitate to show enthusiasm or flash a sense of humor. In this she was similar to her mentor.

The correspondence began on September 28, 1921, while Jeanne was in Milan. Her itinerary took her by way of Venice to Florence, where she spent three weeks, and from where she sent animated descriptions of her experiences to her parents. She then pushed on to Rome, Naples, and Sicily. Throughout her letters, we find remarks that show her preoccupation with psychoanalysis.

On October 17 she discussed the aforementioned H., from The Hague, who would later be her first patient and about whom she wrote her first publication:

> How sad that H. is so moody again; it's regrettable and so depressing. In my heart I really would like to remove her completely from her surroundings and analysis, and from her doctors, and pull her into an entirely different milieu that would enable her to enjoy herself and be young. Is it terrible that I say such a thing? Already I have doubts about analysis; won't it, too, prove to be one-sided, like all human theories? But don't think that I am backing away from Freud; my heart is still drawing me there, and I very much want to get to know completely this deep and expansive discovery. But whether I will become an impassioned analyst?

While in Italy, she read Dante's *Divine Comedy* in Italian and studied the thirteenth-century monk Francis of Assisi and Giotto di Bondone, who portrayed Francis's biography in frescoes.

> Assisi, November 17. . . . I have immersed myself in Francis of Assisi, this powerful figure who has had so much influence through the centuries. He was a great man of his times, although he left no traces behind other than the works created by others who were inspired by his spirit. Do you know anything about him? I would like you to read about him. But actually, you really should see the countryside, the ancient little town where he spent his life in the monastery, and the divine masterpieces by Giotto. . . . I was already well aware of what you write about H.'s analysis; she spends too much time on memories of her youth, and her often irritating attitude toward van Ophuijsen is quite normal and doesn't surprise me. I also think that your opinion is correct in a certain way, that this "annoying friend" is not eager to give up her sessions. A great deal depends on H.'s inner experience of van Ophuijsen as a person. But on the other hand there is in her a strong force that yearns for recovery and the resolution of her problems, and in the end this must

predominate. She also understands her feelings about van Ophuijsen, and that is already a great help. Let us hope that she will succeed. . . . Another analyst seems completely inappropriate, as then everything would have to be gone through from the beginning again, and the transference would necessarily have to develop to the other analyst.

In her letter dated November 29–30, 1921, we can see how much she enjoyed Italy, and especially Rome. She would have liked to stay there longer. As an aside, she ventured an opinion of the Catholic Church:

> What would you think if we stayed here a few short weeks longer; would that be so bad? The money will last us, but I'm sure you will think: Is she never satisfied. . . . We have not gone to see the Pope yet, and I don't feel any great need to do so. I am much more fascinated by the Vatican Museum! . . . [The Catholic Church] had for centuries been so overwhelming and powerful; now it is so squalid, so decrepit, in many respects now just a decrepit facade.

On November 30 she visited San Pietro in Vincoli [Saint Peter in Chains], the site of Michelangelo's renowned marble statue of Moses:

> Today I viewed Moses, marvelous! Enormous and powerful, he fills an entire church. Great suffering, but so lifted above it all, and looking far beyond all earthly affairs.

So much for her observations about the Moses statue. It is unclear whether she knew of Freud's "The Moses of Michelangelo" or of the significance the statue held for Freud, who, since 1901, had gone to see it on numerous occasions. The sculpture is the tomb of Pope Julius II, a circumstance that Freud connected with his brother Julius, who died in infancy. That Freud identified with Moses becomes clear, for example, when he wrote of Pope Julius's sense of kinship with Michelangelo in his attempt "to realize great and mighty ends."[2] This article first appeared anonymously in *Imago* in 1914, and it wasn't until 1927 that Freud disclosed his authorship. Emotionally, Jeanne, too, felt herself on a mission to undertake something great.

Still in Rome, she reported on December 13, 1921, on riots in Vienna, about which she apparently wrote to Freud as well:

> Even here we get unfavorable reports about Vienna; foreigners being accosted, but I live quietly in a room and don't drive out in automobiles wearing a fur coat!

2 Freud, S. (1914). "The Moses of Michelangelo." In *Standard Edition*, vol. XII. London: Hogarth Press, p. 233.

Jeanne's letter from Rome, dated December 20, shows that she had asked Freud to postpone the start of analysis because she wished to stay in Italy for a while longer, but also because she thought that the unrest in Vienna might have abated by then. She also mentioned Carl Gustav Jung[3] by name, but noted that analysis with him would be out of the question. Her comforting words to her father at the end of her Christmas letter are also interesting:

> To my dismay I noticed that it has been an entire week since I have written. But time slides through our hands like an eel, with fearsome speed. Yesterday I wrote to Freud to ask whether he might take me on after Easter because I would much rather start then. But if he were already counting on it or could find no time after Easter, I would come anyway because it is so important to me. I don't want to switch from him to Jung because Jung's method has become completely different.
>
> Actually, I hope that he will have me come at Easter; in my heart that seems the most desirable. I have asked him to respond to me here because we won't be leaving for Naples before Thursday or Friday the 29th or 30th, and I would be able to receive a response here. Once you have received this letter, write me here, and then "poste restante" in Naples. I didn't ask Freud how he views the situation (although I did write him that that is the reason for my desire to postpone), and I fear that he will have little to say about it. . . . I am so happy to get a letter from Father. It's wonderful that you participate in all of my enthusiasms; it's a wonderful feeling. And how pleasant it will be to tell you about everything later, with photos, etc. The reports we get here about Sicily are marvelous, and we hope a little that Freud will postpone! . . . Father, I don't think that you are unreceptive to art, otherwise would you love music or be in agreement with this life of mine? It's just that it's never been developed, always suppressed by others and by concerns of greater import to you. Warm greetings to both of you; write again soon.

Christmas awakened memories of a time when the family was still whole. On December 28 she wrote about a small book that her dear, older

---

3 Carl Gustav Jung (1875–1961) was a Swiss psychiatrist. Freud initially viewed Jung as a potential heir and successor. He also thought that Jung – a non-Jew – could help break down the notion that psychoanalysis was a uniquely Jewish science. However, Freud came to disagree strongly with Jung's emerging concept of a "collective" unconscious, and Jung viewed Freud's theory of the libido as incomplete. A break on theoretical grounds was inevitable. In addition, since before the 1920s, Jung had been attracted to the Völkisch movement in Germany, which was openly anti-Semitic. Although he denied anti-Semitism, in 1934 he could write in the *Zentralblatt fur Psychotherapie*, "The Aryan unconscious has a greater potential than the Jewish unconscious," and "[Freud] knows nothing of the German soul, nor do his followers."

friend, the painter Isaäcson, had sent her, and which she recommended to her mother: "About life after death, where we see those we love again."

In the new year she wrote:

> Naples, January 2, 1922. . . . But now a pleasant little piece of news. I received a letter from Freud this afternoon, forwarded from Rome. (Naturally, I had just sent him a registered express letter on the assumption that a letter had gotten lost!). He writes again, very amiably, that it would work out better for him as well if I came at Easter because in January he doesn't have a single session open, even though I am number 3 on his short list. He says only that the two to three months between Easter and July are too short, and that I would have to return in the fall. If that took up too much of my time, he could arrange analysis for me with someone else. But I responded (in a second registered express letter; he'll have fun with that!), that I'm in no particular hurry, and that I would rather wait until he himself has time for me, in part because I still have to read so much of the literature. He writes about the circumstances in Vienna [Freud's letter of Christmas 1921]: "Your worries are unfounded. . . . Vienna is calm, and foreigners have as little to fear here as, for example, in an Italian city. The riots occurred on one afternoon and haven't been repeated. To the extent that we may predict the future, this worry should be allayed." Emmy R., who is T.'s friend, and who is looking for a room for us, wrote essentially the same thing. Well, because she wrote us that rooms are so terribly hard to come by in Vienna, and that she has found a very good one with a widowed friend of hers, we wrote that we would have to accept it. Now I owe this woman rent for January, that is, 15,000 crowns (which I think is about 6½ guilders, right?) . . . I thought that father would have advised that as well, since given the situation in Vienna, a hotel would not seem acceptable to me. Her name is: Frau Pick, Wollzeile 8, Vienna I.[4]

The letter continues with a lyrical description of the impressions and effects that the trip has had on her. Jeanne and T. spent New Year's Eve reading to each other from Dostoyevsky's *The Idiot* in German.

> Girgenti, January 26, 1922. . . . I'm glad that Freud sent a definitive response that he could take me on in April; nice of him to write immediately. You know, Mother, of course it's going to require diligence and hard work in Vienna, but don't think that analysis is such a terrible thing. . . . I'm healthy and I'm doing it in order to learn the method, so I will feel free to stop at any time. Beyond that, I'm not defending

---

4 The street is in the center of the city, close to St. Stephen's Cathedral.

against difficult moments of resistance with symptoms of illness, because I am healthy. So don't worry about that. In addition, I have acquired such strength, joy, and joie de vivre that I will be able to withstand many shocks. And then again, I have the feeling that I could be content with Freud, but of course that's just an initial impression, but nonetheless I think he will have a great deal of value to impart. What is the course given by Prof. Jelgersma from Leiden?

In her next letter she shows how envious she is of her mother's classical gymnasium education with Latin and Greek; in her high school, although she had learned physics, biology, and chemistry, she had only been taught modern languages: French, German, and English. It is also notable that she concluded the letter with a warm hug, signing it "your youngest," by which she claimed the place of her 3½-year-old younger sister, who had died in May 1901:

> Syracuse, February 2, 1922. Syracuse is full of ancient history, . . . With all its ancient stories of heroes and gods and great men who lived there. I would so much have liked to know about all of them! Unfortunately, I doubly miss a classical education, which I so much would have liked to have had. . . . What a wonderful, raw power these ancients had! Today we recall with horror: "inhuman" and "cruel," the slave-driving, the human slaughter and razing of cities and plundering. What would the ancients have said if they could have seen our twentieth century, so full of war with its sophisticated and insane implements of murder? . . . I'll stop with these stories from this ancient land, although there is still much to be told. But I'm sure you know more about it than I do. If we start to travel together again, I'll be able to show you lots of things, so many happy memories, lovely little places! I will be with you in my thoughts on the 8th [her mother's birthday] . . . And I hug you and Papa so very warmly as your youngest.

Jeanne took up H.'s analysis again in the following letter. It seems that she was again considering analyzing her herself once she was in Vienna. She wrote her mother from Taormina on February 3, 1922:

> Of course your letters are full of H.; I can well understand why you are brooding and empathizing with her difficulties. . . . At the moment I have the feeling that she needs peace during the analysis, in the hope that she will complete it. Once it concludes, or if in the end she needs to terminate, then get out for a time, somewhere completely different, with many new impressions and with one activity or another; in the worst case come with me to Vienna, although it is somewhat eerie there. So for that reason there would be a lot going on there that might

get her out of her brooding. I would very much like to try it with her, although I will have a great deal of work during this time, but I think that I could risk it, and that I'd have the courage and strength needed. The only thing is that she would have had to leave analysis herself, with or without favorable results.

In her final letter from Italy, she noted that she found it difficult to leave. In it she wrote about a period of depression during her medical studies and her doubts back then about her choice of profession:

Taormina, February 13, 1922. . . . We will leave here tomorrow, a difficult farewell, but I have a wonderfully gratifying and rich feeling about everything that I enjoyed and experienced during this half-year. It will be wonderful to come home again and tell you something about it (even though it cannot yet be very much), and it is also a pleasant feeling to go back to work, and to transform all that I have gathered into something active. I hope that I will have the courage to accept my daily life and my discipline, both of which had seemed so insurmountably difficult for so long.

Jeanne's second series of letters comprise a period of more than one year. They were largely sent from Vienna between April 18, 1922, and April 30, 1923. The letters begin with a description of her first meeting with Freud:

Vienna, April 18, 1922. Dear Father and Mother, my first visit with Freud took place this afternoon. He is exactly as I had imagined him, slim, with a sharply-defined, gray head and beautifully expressive hands. He was very amiable; he is going to look for a room for me, or better said, have someone look around for me. I now go to see him once each day, alternating with two colleagues between 5–6, 6–7, 7–8 o'clock in the evening. We alternate because otherwise one of us would never be able to go to the theater or a concert. That seems to be a necessary part of it! Freud recommends that we not begin right away with real psychiatric training, rather that we wait for a time. So for now I will have enough time for museums, reading, and not to forget: for my piano which, as an aside, I like very much. . . . Have discovered, unfortunately, that my hotel is not located in the Votivplatz but in the Freiheitsplatz, and I hope that the post office understands that because I very much look forward to a report. . . . Hugs to all of you from Jeanne.

In her second letter from Vienna, she described the depressed postwar atmosphere of the city. After her search for lodgings, she decided that she would in fact take the room at Wollzeile 8. She was enthusiastic about her analysis. How she anticipated defending Freud's analysis fee – in Dutch guilders – is interesting:

> Vienna, April 21, 1922. . . . another world . . ., one sees a lot of invalids and crippled beggars, many pale faces, emaciated by hunger . . .. The generally nice clothing is notable; girls in nicely fitting shoes and dressed more or less fashionably, although the way they look makes one want to give them a couple of slices of bread-and-butter. Of course, in the hotels and restaurants you can get all kinds of good things (perhaps not milk, I don't know), but for the Viennese it must be horrifically expensive. . . . Freud gave me an address, but it turned out that the apartment won't be free until the summer. I then went to see Frau Pick; the room there is not taken at the moment . . .. So for the time being my address is: c/o Frau Pick, Wollzeile 8 (third floor), Vienna I. . . . I went to the opera yesterday (*The Valkyrie*), that is, the last two acts because I was with Freud until 6 and it had already started at 6. . . . The analytical work is extraordinarily interesting, but difficult at times as well. It couldn't be otherwise, but my assessment will come much later, of course. So, now to the financial matter, which I hope won't frighten you too much. Freud was surprised that I didn't know because I had not inquired by letter; it was also my fault that I completely forgot about it. That you know. He charges just as he had before the war, 50 crowns or 25 florin per session, and he would like to have it paid in guilders on a bank in The Hague. It is a lot, but he is right actually. I hope that Papa won't find it too terrible; but he also granted me the trips to Paris and Italy, so if he now understands that I am certain in my feeling that this is the direction I must go in, and that I need this analysis for my future work, then I hope that he will agree to this as well. I firmly believe that this is not money poured down the drain.

From the following letter, it is even clearer that Jeanne was depressed during the final year of her medical studies; the "loss of interest" that she wrote about may be consistent with that. In her analysis, too, she spoke of a period of depression, but that related to her at 17.

> Vienna, Thursday, April 27, 1922. . . . Things continue to go well; I am extremely interested in my work, and I am so happy that my interest in scientific matters has been rekindled. I imagined that I had lost that during my final year of study; but I think that I lived out my emotional life in Paris and Italy to such an extent that now . . . I will again be interested in my subject area. Freud is very kind, simply a happy man, and every once in a while there is something for us to laugh about together. That is good compensation for the difficult moments. In addition, when things get hard, he always knows how

to encourage me with just the right word so that things work out by themselves. . . . It's no wonder that, given the current circumstances, he thinks we're loaded; he knows that I spent 4 months in Paris and half a year traveling through Italy and was in no hurry to begin my studies. Furthermore, I don't think he distinguishes; there are always other psychoanalysts to whom one could go, and I think that he simply stands by his fee. His time is also very valuable. In the meantime, I'm very thankful for Father's notes and his philosophical attitude: "I don't think that it's poured down the drain; it's transferred from my account into his." I also don't think that Freud will waste it, especially since in the meantime I learn so much as a result! . . . Life here certainly isn't cheap anymore; the prices have pretty much overtaken the [value of the] currency. Everyday things are still somewhat less expensive for those of us with the highest currency, the highest-hard-currency people [because of the Dutch guilders]; other things are about the same, insanely expensive for the Viennese.

In the next letter she mentioned an English friend of Freud's, probably Ernest Jones, who is mentioned by name in a later letter. The birthdays of her deceased sisters take place during this time; her youngest sister on May 7, her oldest on May 21. She mentioned this in connection with a performance of Mahler's *Songs on the Death of Children*:

Vienna, May 2, 1922. . . . Yesterday (May 1) was a Sunday, so there was no mail. (Yes, of course I worked! And Freud as well; it's a working Sunday!). . . . I enclose Freud's invoice, which he always writes out on the first of the month. Will Father pay it; it is made out in the name of his English friend. Send me a note whether it worked. Now to your question: yes, I live only ¼ hour from Freud, so I can walk. I'm not taking other courses, but I am reading a lot of literature. I've attended a meeting of the Psychoanalytical Society, but I think I already mentioned that, so nothing further on the subject for now. They happen every 14 days. Analysis takes up a lot of time, sometimes a little less. In any event, my interest in the city, people, art, piano, etc. has not diminished, and I'm still enjoying as many of the beautiful and important things as before. My interest in the subject has reasserted itself; what more could I want . . .. A mediocre Mahler concert: *Songs of a Wayfarer*, *Songs on the Death of Children*, *First Symphony*. So, everything was familiar and beautiful. Mother, you will get this letter on about the 7th, one of the hard May days.[5]

5 Hard days because two of her sisters died in May.

The next letter has no date, but it was probably the follow-up to the letter of May 7. In it, she described a "lovely day outside" with blossoming trees and beautiful vistas overlooking the beckoning misty blue mountains. She asked her mother to do something for an acquaintance, perhaps hoping that looking after another person might ease her mother's memory of loss. She described the furnishings in her room as "not uncomfortable, but the photos from Italy are an improvement." She wrote again on May 11:

> Vienna, May 11. Dear Mother, . . . Now to answer your question. The Psychoanalytical Society meets every 14 days, so it met yesterday evening, which was the second time for me. Naturally, it was somewhat more pleasant than the first time, because finding myself suddenly among 40–50 strange people isn't anything I enjoy. It's very interesting, especially to see all of the types. Of course there are many peculiar ones, many of them slightly crazy!, male and female of all ages and nationalities, mostly Viennese, of course, but also Americans, English, a couple of Swiss, Germans. I'm the only Dutch person. Naturally some very interesting fellow students, a few less pleasant ones. And among the analysts there are also some mediocre people! The first time I realized this was at a very important lecture given by Dr. Rank, who is certainly a special person. But of the rest whom I have heard so far, most appear not able even to stand in Freud's shadow, but that probably holds true everywhere and with everybody. I have made the acquaintance of one of Freud's nieces, who offered to help me find my way in the concert and operatic life of Vienna (because it's very difficult to get tickets if you don't have connections; everything is usually sold out!). And I'll probably go out into the countryside with her, or something like that. I also spoke to one of his daughters, but only briefly. Beyond that, making acquaintances is difficult, and there is so little time, and as Freud told me earlier, laughingly: nationals of each country crawl into their own little corner, Americans with Americans, etc.! I'd have to have a little corner just to myself . . .. And now you want to know what people in Vienna think about psychoanalysis. I don't have much experience with that yet: Frau Pick, who knew Freud superficially from before, says that he and his theory had certainly made an impression for a time, but now command less attention again. But, as she admitted quite honestly at the outset, she herself doesn't know anything about it. I once spoke to a young lawyer who was a bit derisive, as if talking about some trifling foolishness. I asked him whether he had read anything about it. He answered, "I once read *The Interpretation of Dreams*, and well yes, it gets talked about!" In plain language: he doesn't know a thing, or more to the point, he's heard rumors about it. That seems to be how it generally is here, just as it is abroad and in our country as well: a lot of resistance and enmity from those who don't know anything

about it or don't want to know. But it always amuses me how people react. The R.'s didn't know anything, but recently the wife heard that it must be "terribly interesting," but what she knew about it was quite strange. Naturally, there is a fairly large school for analysis; there are quite a few non-physicians among them.

Jeanne's mother began to read Freud's writings, and Jeanne warned her that to really understand what psychoanalysis means one must practice it. She then followed with a careful interpretation of her mother's "repressed" pain, and then hinted at her own "slightly neurotic condition" and how depressed she was at 17 or 18. It is here that Multatuli is mentioned, a friend of her mother's family whom Freud also greatly respected.[6] In the same letter she advised her mother to use her experience to "enlighten the grandchildren about the mysteries of birth," as her sister was pregnant with her second child at the time:

> Friday, May 26. . . . It's very good that you've started with Freud, but Mother, don't think that because you've heard five lectures by Jelgersma and read a book by Freud that you know something about it. I've been working at it for quite a while, and I discover again and again just *how much* literature there is and *how little* I know. . . . I'm only now beginning to understand *something* of psychoanalysis from the practical exercises that I do on myself, from daily sessions with Freud, and from reading the copious literature. . . . Why are you so resisting the distress of your children? Are you yourself so frightened of it? Sorrow is necessary in order to experience happiness later. Then again, staying stuck in sorrow is a necessity for many, which, however, dissolves when one *really* recognizes that one comes to inner understanding not by reason alone.[7] Don't worry about me; I'm now contented and happy. If you were to ask my acquaintances here, they would all say that I'm healthy and cheerful, and that sometimes I even infect others! Frau Pick asks whether I ever get nervous! She wouldn't have believed my mild state of

6 Multatuli (Latin: I have suffered [or borne] much) was the *nom de plume* of the Dutch writer Eduard Douwes Dekker (1820–1887). In 1906 Freud took part in a survey by the Viennese publisher Hugo Heller, asking writers and scientists to "name ten good books." Freud "assumed that Heller meant books that were like 'good' friends, to whom one owes a part of one's knowledge of life and the view of the world, books which one has enjoyed oneself and gladly commends to others." He placed Multatuli's letters and books at the top of this list. *Freud's Library. A Comprehensive Catalogue/Freuds Bibliothek. Vollständiger Katalog.* (Davies, K. & Fichtner, G. [2006]. London: The Freud Museum London/Tübingen: edition diskord, p 30.

7 Jeanne's rivalry with her mother apparently related not only to the latter's classical education, but to emotions such as distress and sorrow.

neurosis at 17 and 18, when I could do little more than cry and be depressed and fearful! . . . Listen, you shouldn't think that I didn't find Multatuli lovely back then; I've always greatly respected him (probably also because of you). I always found *Max Havelaar* and *Woutertje Pieterse* [Little Walter Pieterse] magnificent, and his *Ideas*[8] as well (what I know of them). But I know so little about him and read him too early to understand the full scope of what he was saying. Freud cites him in one of his smaller texts as a "great thinker and friend of humanity" (an open letter to someone who was asking him about the sexual enlightenment of children).[9] He is far too little known, Freud told me. . . . I'll cite for you what Freud quoted from Dekker [Multatuli]: "In general, my feeling is that some things remain far too concealed. It is right to keep children's fantasy pure, but this purity is not maintained by ignorance. It seems to me, rather, that keeping something hidden from boys and girls makes them doubt the truth even more. Out of curiosity one tries to track down things which, if they were told to us without much fuss, would be of little or no interest. If this ignorance could be preserved, I might reconcile myself to it, but it is impossible; children come into contact with other children and read books that cause them to reflect. It is the secrecy with which parents treat what has in fact been understood that increases the appetite, satisfying it only in part and only in secret. This heats the heart and corrupts fantasy; the child already sins, but the parents continue to believe that their child doesn't know what sin is."[10]

Freud continues: "I don't know how one could say it any better, but perhaps a few things could be added." And then he discusses his scientific discoveries, naturally grounded in the perceptions of a practicing physician. You must read that sometime. Let Miek read it as well, and do try to persuade her that she should enlighten Adri and tell him the truth in the most ordinary and simple way. Don't think that a child notices nothing when their mother is pregnant! They notice *everything*, in any case the intelligent ones do, and they fantasize about it. Don't let Adri's brother remain a mystery for her the way Jootje was. He is sensible enough to understand!

In her next letter, she shared with her mother her newly acquired understandings and even complimented her mother on her progress. She wrote

---

8 *Max Havelaar, Woutertje Pieterse,* and *Ideas* are a few of Multatuli's works.
9 Multatuli [Pseudonym of Eduard Douwes Dekker]. (1899). *Auswahl aus seinen Werken.* Translated from the Dutch by Wilhelm Spohr. Minden: Bruns Verlag.
10 The quote comes from one of Multatuli's letters to his fiancée "Everdine" (Tine, Everdina H. van Wijnbergen).

about Anna Freud's maiden speech on the occasion of her becoming a member of the Viennese Psychoanalytical Society:

> June 1, 1922. Dear mother. . . . I can well understand that you have a lot of questions about Freud's book. You are slowly learning to understand psychoanalysis. It's not simple. Remember that he himself has worked on it for 30 to 40 years to bring it to this level. Your remark, that analysands, especially those who are neurotic, prefer to present fantasies rather than realities, is completely correct. Freud would say, "A very sensible question" (although it was in regard to a different question that I had asked him). Only practice has demonstrated that this difference is completely meaningless for the analysis and treatment of neurotics; in fact, it's not the *facts* that cause a neurosis, but the collision between unsatisfied drives and reality, a collision that gets expressed so nicely in fantasies and daydreams. For example, it's not so important whether masturbation (a frequent cause of neurosis) during puberty[11] is in fact practiced or only fantasized about, because the result is the same: repression of both the reality and the actual deed[12] can lead to neurosis. These fantasies must be uncovered in treatment; what the patient talks about in analysis originates in his unconscious and leads ineluctably back to these childhood fantasies. It makes no difference whether something additional is fantasized or is subtracted . . .. Yesterday evening Freud's daughter gave a lecture at the Society. It concerned a limited subject,[13] but the way she told it was very clear and engaging. It was nice to see how much the two of them like each other; it shows in everything. She is exactly my age but looks much younger. . . . [Written in the margin:] In September (I think 24, 25, and 26) there will be an [International] Psychoanalytic Congress in Berlin, which I would like to attend!

It turned out that on the evening before summer vacations, which were to last until the end of September, Jeanne decided to spend another year in Vienna in order to conclude her training there. She was able to do this

---

11 An obsolete theory, but one that was current at the time.

12 This was a mistake on her part; what she undoubtedly meant was "of both the reality and the fantasy."

13 The "limited subject" that Anna Freud discussed in her maiden speech turned out to be an important addition to psychoanalytic theory, which she developed in cooperation with Lou Andreas Salomé, her esteemed psychoanalytic mother. The title of her maiden speech, "Beating Fantasies and Daydreams," was a revision of her father's article "A Child is Being Beaten." The English translation appeared in the 1923 *International Journal of Psycho-Analysis*, vol 4, 89–102. It is reprinted in Young-Bruehl, E. (1988). *Anna Freud. A Biography*. New York: Summit Books, pp. 103–105.

because a psychoanalytic polyclinic had opened in Vienna after the one in Berlin.

> Thursday, June 29 and Sunday, July 2, 1922., 8 a.m. Dear mother, . . . Today is my final day with Freud. . . . I will tell you about my last conversations with him later because otherwise this letter would get too long. A psychoanalytic Ambulatorium opened here recently so I won't have to travel to Berlin, which has many advantages. I will most likely stay here for at least one year. I have bought a number of books, about which I am very happy; it's not complete yet as at the moment I am missing several volumes, but the Psychoanalytischer Verlag is going to try to get used copies. For us it's actually terribly inexpensive, an entire bookcase full for barely 30 florin!

Jeanne attended her first International Congress in Berlin after her vacation in 1922. This is probably where she first met Hans Lampl, although she didn't mention this in her letters.

> Berlin, Tuesday afternoon, September 26, 1922. . . . It is a strange thing, such a Congress, absolutely nothing for Fräulein Doktor, your daughter. But in any case very amusing and luckily often very interesting. The lectures from 9 to 1 and from 4 to 7 are outstanding!! Luckily I have this afternoon off because that's when the business meeting, which is closed to guests, takes place. But I have to say that by yesterday evening I was completely exhausted. There were about 250 attendees (about 150 members and 100 guests), so, a lot of people, and, you understand, the strangest jumbled mix, it paid to look at all the oddities, all possible races, Germans, Austrians, Swiss, English, Americans, Italians, Hungarians, Indians, even a Hindu woman, all in all quite interesting. There was a reception on Sunday evening; I have to admit that we were impressively received by the Berliners, especially given the present situation. It was more than full this morning when Freud spoke. Happily there were also other interesting speakers in various areas. Some were more boring, of course. Freud hasn't been in Vienna for the past three months, but he considers a direct danger to be very improbable; food and coal deliveries are worse, but if the situation worsens, he plans to move away with his worldly goods. So we'll just have to wait; the whole thing doesn't seem all that bad to me. It seems to me that the food problem is tolerable if one has money. Here things don't appear rosy either, but nothing in comparison with Vienna. I will now go and have supper with a group of Congress attendees with whom I already had lunch today. On days like this you have to focus solely on the Congress. On Saturday and Sunday I enjoyed the Egyptians, Rembrandt, and the old Flemish masters. The pieces are magnificent, and there are so many! But right now I'm

completely focused on psychoanalysis. There will be a banquet for everyone tomorrow evening, the only official celebration. I'm curious to see whether there will be a lot more "speechifying." And on Thursday evening I will travel directly back to Vienna for a number of reasons: first, I'm going to be a bit overwound from the whole thing and have little desire to drag myself through the city (and two days are too short anyway). Second, Freud will hold a meeting for the various students on Saturday afternoon, and although I don't have to be there, I would like to anyway. And third, I'd like to spend quiet time at home until I start to work again. So on Friday afternoon I'll be back at Wollzeile and begin again with a fresh spirit. . . . (Here in Berlin there are even three female psychoanalysts and one female non-physician.) One of them held a good lecture here yesterday; I hope that I'll be able to speak with her this evening. . . . Freud understood your worries completely, but of course he can't foresee the future, although he doesn't consider it as dangerous as Father does.

At this time she apparently received the news that her mother had developed heart problems. Here, too, Jeanne gave free rein to her newly acquired knowledge and "interpreted" these problems as a sign of loving and worry. Jeanne then wrote about her own difficult phase of analysis, which she called the "crux." She distinguished between her actual treatment and the "training portion" of the analysis, as if these were clearly distinguishable phases. During this time, finances remained an important point in her correspondence with her father.

Vienna, Monday, October 2, 1922. Dear Father and Mother, . . . Outwardly everything is exactly as it was before, except that the prices have increased about tenfold. Freud began again this morning; I now have sessions from 10–11 in the morning, which is much better than the early afternoon sessions. . . . I think that things don't look so happy for you emotionally? Oh Moedertje,[14] if you only understood the secret pathways by which it goes back into the past, an idea such as yours that you must die in your 60th year from heart disease just like your father! Your great love for him and your great similarities are no reason that destiny promises you the same death. None of us can evade destiny, but you really don't have much reason to worry. Your heart may not be completely healthy, but with mild symptoms like yours a person can live to be 90 or 100. . . . I don't know whether Vienna with its rain and muddy streets and all of the impoverished, pale faces of troubled people might not be even gloomier than Schiedam. I'm not having things easy at the moment; my analysis is at the crux of all

14 The Dutch diminutive of Mother.

my difficulties and conflicts, and it is not a pleasant stage, but when this has been surmounted, the personal portion of the analysis will be over and I will then devote myself completely and exclusively to the training portion. That is a consolation; beyond that I am firmly convinced that it is necessary to overcome everything in order to be a fully adequate person, and that is necessary if one wishes to cure others and help them along.

I haven't discussed the polyclinic with Freud yet, and I think I will wait until the difficulties have been resolved. For the first week I have enough to do with my own analysis + that of H.[15]

Vienna, October 27, 1922. . . . It is terribly cold here, a few days of nice weather, but today horrible dirty wet snow, cold wind, and slush, unpleasantly shivery. I have to go and buy some woolen socks. Father, could you send me 200 florin? As of November 1, Frau Pick has to increase the rent, which I can understand because everything is becoming more expensive. It will then go up to 2.50 florin. That's still only 75 florin a month. Naturally, fire and light are extra.

Jeanne wrote dismissively of Freud's "little invoice." His request that the amount be transferred to Ernest Jones in England is understandable given the enormous currency devaluation.

Vienna, November 1, 1922. . . . Enclosed is Freud's little invoice. Father, you remember the bank, right? And on Jones's account. Freud asked me about it, and I answered that I thought that it wouldn't be any trouble for Papa to transfer it. I hope that that is so.

Her parents apparently had questions regarding the results of Jeanne's costly training. She gave a masterful defense of her analysis. Here again she expressed her goal of returning to the Netherlands after concluding her training in order to open a "small children's clinic" or open a psychoanalytic practice of her own:

Vienna, November 7, 1922. . . . A considerable piece of difficult analysis has been surmounted, but it's not yet finished. . . . I'm a little impatient because things like this sometimes go slowly and require time, and of course I have no right to think that things would go faster for me, all the more so because there is so much material that I have strongly defended against. I really want to do it thoroughly (thus requiring patience) because I am convinced of the deep importance and great

---

15 H. was Jeanne's Dutch acquaintance who was now apparently in analysis with her, perhaps because van Ophuijsen was in Berlin at the time for his own training analysis with Karl Abraham.

value of a thorough analysis. And finally, as an analyst one must be up to the challenge of knowing and understanding oneself as much as possible. The latter gives me joy and confidence in the face of all difficulties.

There are now evening courses four times a week at the polyclinic. Yesterday I heard some fairly interesting things from Dr. Bernfeld, who isn't a doctor but a pedagogue or something similar. It was about child psychology and the psychology of educators and education. An exceptional person and outstanding speaker, which is also worth a lot. Not all of it is equally interesting, but I pursue everything nonetheless, because this is my training period, and later I won't have the opportunity to listen to lectures, and so I have to be able to do everything alone. Who knows what might become of a small children's clinic, but in Holland I probably won't get a lot of help with it. In addition, I think that my scientific interest will be directed more toward a larger psychoanalytic practice. But that's all still up in the air.

In her letters Jeanne regularly wrote about playing the piano. She defended analysis in a passionate plea, apparently after her mother ventured a criticism in one of her letters. She noted that her writings might actually be published. In the following letter she let her mother know about her plans regarding upcoming publications:

Vienna, November 14 and 15, 1922. . . . I just studied a piece by Beethoven, which was soothing, something I hadn't done recently. I now take a number of courses; every evening except Saturday, one or two hours. So there's a lot going on. Z.'s article offers little that is new. As the Viennese would put it, "soup logic with dumpling arguments." This from someone who of course had never thoroughly examined the "coarse and unscientific method" and is motivated purely by feelings. There is no way to argue scientifically against this. . . . The fact that when relating their dreams patients change things and add fantasies is known to all analysts. But that means little; all thoughts associated with the dream are connected to it, and the life of fantasy is just as important for patients, if not more so, than the events themselves. In other words, whether one analyzes the dream or the associated fantasy makes absolutely no difference for curing the patient. In addition, a consciously intended lie will be immediately exposed, and then have its own special significance for getting to know the patient's character. Well, I could write you much more about this interesting subject, but at some point I have to stop. The fact that there are many people, both physicians and laypeople, who fake analysis for fun and enjoy it simply as sensation really says nothing about the scientific truth of Freud's long years of work. At most one could say that it points to the unethical and immoral consequences of the repressions brought about by our culture. Those who are more familiar with Freud and with analysis truly do not doubt the highly ethical aspirations of both. Naturally, many might be apt to tell you that you are operating under Freud's suggestion and are therefore not without prejudice. The only thing that I can answer is that they must experience it themselves, and only then will they be able to judge, and realize that "suggestion" (does anyone who uses this word even know what it means?) cannot long withstand analysis. An imputation that is really unfounded dissolves sooner or later because it cannot retain its power in a vacuum. It suddenly occurs to me that I could almost send this turn of phrase to the newspaper!! Luckily it's not necessary; that which has real value will hold its ground on its own. . . . The work is still wonderful.

It is possible that Jeanne's mother tried to rein in her daughter's idealizing tendencies. Jeanne seems to have only partly accepted what she said, and at the same time disclosed her "ambitious" plans to write something better than "fruitless newspaper polemics."

Vienna, November 20, 1922. Dear mother, . . . Are you already such a Freudian that you write *prêcher le converti* [preaching to the converted]? I didn't know; have you been reading a lot of his work? Another book of his has just been translated into Dutch: *Beyond the Pleasure Principle* with the somewhat strange translation: *Het levensmysterie en de psychoanalyse* [The Mystery of Life and Psychoanalysis]. But you'll be able to read it better in German anyway; if you want I can send it to you. I already know that a quickly jotted down exposé, as in my previous letter, is not fit to print in a newspaper! I don't think that I'm capable of arguing with a sophisticated journalist, and I presumably will never get involved with that! But if I were to write something really good, then my ambition would be directed at something other than a priori useless and fruitless newspaper polemics! . . . I now have to go to my course, three in a row, and I won't get home for dinner until 9:45. The daily agenda is peculiar. But one gets used to everything. And now the day. The weather is the worst possible, biting wind and dirty, dirty snow. Hugs from Jeanne.

The argument between mother and daughter may actually have veiled something deeper. Her mother may have sensed what was at issue: her daughter will develop and disentangle from the work of mourning that they share. It is possible that Jeanne's excuses for the cost of analysis may – apart from the reality – also have masked her feelings of guilt about the separation.

Vienna, November 27, 1922. . . . I'm not familiar with Zullinger's little book. "From Zurich" does not necessarily mean that it is Jungian;

there are certainly real analysts in the Freudian sense in Zurich. And Jung and his followers aren't necessarily stating falsehoods. To a certain extent their views are congruent with Freud's psychoanalysis, although they have often coined different words for previously known phenomena and also "rediscovered" some things that Freud discovered decades ago, to which they then give nice sounding names. The only crucial points where they really diverge concern the origins of psychoanalysis, namely the recognition that each neurosis begins in childhood, with the conclusion that thorough analysis is necessary from childhood into early adolescence. Jung reformulated all of the discoveries with regard to the child's emotional life and rationalized them at a "more pleasant" level. What is remarkable is that someone who actually understood something about the analytical discoveries could then later negate them so completely. This is no unqualified parroting of Freud; it is completely clear from his own writings. You write about "your belief in psychoanalysis," and then, "a belief that it could benefit humanity." The latter sounds very nice, but who knows whether anything will or can ever bring a "benefit"? Analysis was born of experience and even more so of the *necessity of the age*, just as logically as all intellectual currents. What is good and what is bad? Analysis is *necessary*, and necessary means that our fallen humanity recognizes its spiritual needs just as much, and probably even more, urgently than the material needs, because understanding and self-knowledge are necessary to solve the material side of the problem of our century. Analysis teaches people to know themselves, to observe their drives and motives matter-of-factly and objectively, thereby freeing all energy that had until then been bound up for use in the pursuit of higher goals. How many, and to what extent, higher goals are pursued depends on the person and the possibilities that present themselves. The same will hold true of humanity once it has, over the decades, learned to see psychoanalysis as something true and necessary. Freud was ahead of humanity by many decades; we followers perhaps by a few [decades]; however, in 20–30 years (optimists say 10) all psychiatrists, physicians, educators, parents, and perhaps even the leaders of parties and states, will recognize the necessity for analytic training. Whether this will lead to something better and happier is another story; in the end, humanity has remained what it is throughout the centuries, but it is *necessary* and *inevitable*. What do you mean by "belief"? In analytic terminology it would be rendered approximately as "transference." That is of course the way in which all of us, Freud's students, learn analysis from him (directly or from others or from books). But one can test the facts out on oneself. And if one learns more about oneself every day (not just by being told, but rather *sees*, *feels*, and *experiences*), which is what he discovered years ago, then "belief" falls away, at least as such. If it has withstood the test of practical perception, one must accept it as objective fact. Personally, analysis makes me happy because it is freeing. Is there anything more beautiful than understanding and probing the life of the mind? And so I am grateful, even when it is hard and requires patience and persistence, especially when someone like me brings a good bit of neurosis to the table. On the other hand, there's an advantage to a selective way of learning about it. At the moment I'm reading Shakespeare in English. Difficult! [She then writes about the icy wind, clothing, and about her costly analysis.] And I'm so sinfully expensive! But I don't think it's just a luxury! It's essential for my work, and it is a blessing for me.

She planned to celebrate St. Nicholas Day on December 5, in the evening, with a small group of people in the Dutch manner with little presents. She also reported on concerts and opera performances she had attended, and concluded with an almost symbolic sentence:

Vienna, December 2, 1922. . . .. Next week I hope to hear the *Magic Flute*, and then *Don Juan* will be performed.

She continued her defense of analysis, supporting her position by citing Freud's thoughts and statements, either from the literature or from what he told her during her analysis. But she also wrote that she increasingly liked to write about theoretical aspects of psychoanalysis. She also cautiously ventured her psychoanalytic views on art, a territory in which Freud felt very comfortable.

When she received one of her rare letters from her father, she interpreted it humorously as a traditional surprise gift from St. Nick:

Tuesday, December 5, 1922. Dear Father and Mother, a letter from Father is always a surprise, and I should actually have it framed in gold! But I'm very happy about it, and also about the interest both of you are taking in psychoanalysis. Naturally I have a lot of comments. This morning I had a conversation with Freud about your letter. What always gives me the most confidence are two things upon which his working method is grounded:

1. How cautiously he uses his ample experience to construct the theory; and
2. His own skepticism regarding all theorizing. I've already written you about the first point; psychoanalysis is a science of experience, and naturally a theory is indispensable as a working hypothesis. But Freud is very skeptical of any theory that deviates to whatever extent from immediate perception, and he is prepared to drop any theory if experience proves it false.

I asked him how often in his long working life he had had to discard a theory. He answered that it happened only once. I can tell mother about this because I think she knows enough theory. Freud originally thought that the sexual abuse of children by adults was a frequent cause of hysterical symptoms. Later it became crystal clear that this seduction never occurred in reality, but was constructed based on (partially unconscious) fantasies on the part of the patient. In practical terms, these fantasies have the same psychic significance for patients, and they are exactly as pathogenic as actual experience. Thus, discovering them and bringing them to consciousness are the same in the therapeutic sense. Naturally, there is a great difference only in theory.[16]

Other changes in psychoanalysis that have occurred over the years are merely expansions, deepenings, or shifts that do not overthrow the original construct, but have enlarged and expanded it. This morning Freud made the comparison with an Italian Renaissance church, which over the years (centuries) has been transformed so that the original church has become the transept and a nave has had to be built onto it. In this way the space was enlarged, but the original core remains. The fact that he was forced to reject only one theory testifies to the caution with which he works. Freud has often been reproached for the reformulations and changes; he himself views them as necessities for a true science. To him, that is the difference between belief and scientific conviction. The former is an incontrovertible something that the believer views as the indisputable and absolute truth; the willingness to replace one theory by another when it proves necessary testifies to a scientific spirit.

Now I'm going to give you several quotations from his 1920 *Beyond the Pleasure Principle*. In it he speaks of life and death <u>instincts</u>, much of which he views as "speculation." He writes:

"On the other hand it should be made quite clear that the uncertainty of our speculation has been greatly increased by the necessity for borrowing from the science of biology. Biology is truly a land of unlimited possibilities. We may expect it to give us the most surprising information and we cannot guess what answers it will return in a few dozen years to the questions we have put to it. <u>They may be of a kind which will blow away the whole of our artificial structure of hypotheses</u>.[17] If so, it may be asked why I have embarked upon

---

16 Since then, the uncomfortable reality of widespread sexual abuse – and not only in Catholic institutions – has rendered this theory obsolete.

17 Jeanne de Groot's underlining.

such a line of thought as the present one, and in particular why I have decided to make it public. Well – I cannot deny that some of the analogies, correlations and connections which it contains seemed to me to deserve consideration."[18]

(It's a very interesting little work that points toward many perspectives and paths). And he continues:

"This in turn raises a host of other questions to which we can at present find no answer. We must be patient and await fresh methods and occasions of research. We must also be ready to abandon a path that we have followed for a time if it seems to be leading to no good end. Only believers, who demand that science shall be a substitute for the catechism they have given up, will blame an investigator for developing or even transforming his views. We may also take comfort for the slow advances of our scientific knowledge in the words of the poet (Rückert in the "Maqama of Hariri"):[19]

'What we cannot reach flying we must reach limping . . .. The Book tells us it is no sin to limp.' "[20]

So really, dear father, Freud is no blind slave to theory. Naturally, there are followers who would prefer it if he were, but there's nothing that can be done about that.

Jeanne concluded this theoretical discussion about the life and death instincts with something that Freud told her during her analysis:

This morning Freud told me that several of his followers view psychoanalysis as a messianic gospel and expect that it will suddenly appear in humanity in that form as "the Salvation." That's nonsense, of course; psychoanalysis must penetrate and become assimilated slowly. It isn't finished yet; it has gaps, and that is also its fascination, which will perhaps be lessened in 20 years when it has become a completed whole. But by then it will have also gone much more into the public domain. A period of 10 years, which the optimist Bernfeld (a young educator and analyst, very interesting and a talented person) has cited, seems to Freud to be too short, even though analysis has made enormous strides in the 10 years since 1912. But of course there is no way to predetermine such a time period, as it depends on a thousand factors. In my opinion, what we need to do is continue along the path of experience, always testing the theory until it really has

18 Freud, S. (1920). "Beyond the Pleasure Principle." In *Standard Edition*, vol. XXIII. London: Hogarth, p. 60.
19 Friedrich Rückert (1788–1866) was a German poet. An Orientalist, he translated the "Maqamat of Al-Hariri of Basra," and wrote in that style.
20 Freud, S. (1920). Op. cit., pp. 63–64.

no gaps. For that to happen, deepenings, associations, and reformulations will be necessary, but Freud's results to date give us confidence
that not much will have to be rejected. – As far as the brooding of
neurotics is concerned, this accusation is not aimed at analysis. Neurotics brood a priori, and that is their illness, that they cannot reconcile
themselves to reality and must satisfy themselves in their fantasy life.
Analysis doesn't produce brooding, although it may perhaps poten-
tiate and provoke it for a time, but in the end it pulls the libidinous
forces (unused until then) into reality. Of course this does not happen with all neurotic patients, but that is no argument against what is
valuable in analysis. – I could write much more, but I will conclude for
the time being. If you're interested I'll write more later.

I just received both packages, how nice! Such a quantity of sur-
prises. And exactly on December 5. This evening the four of us will
celebrate together! I have to go now and conclude in a hurry. Farewell!
Hugs to both of you from Jeanne. No time to correct, unfortunately!
Please forgive all mistakes.

Vienna, January 20, 1923. Received your letter this morning. Wonderful that you so enjoyed the *St. Matthew Passion* and Wüllner.[21] . . .
I very much doubt whether I understand more of Goethe than you or
anyone else. You are right, of course, that I have recently viewed art dif-
ferently and from a psychological and scientific perspective. But there
are other ways to understand art, and why should those be of any less
value than the analytical. Naturally it's different, and once you have
penetrated into the deepest motives of the soul, you won't any longer
be satisfied with another method, will find it superficial, and seek to
understand more deeply. But for another person, whose attitude is not
analytical, the aesthetic pleasure, the purely emotional response has
exactly as much value. Yes, the passage "rest gently" has always been a
mystery to me as well. I feel that it sounds as from a powerful primeval
voice, over and beyond everything, but not as *loud* and direct as it does
frequently. I have no idea why that is. I will go and work at the polyclinic as soon as it is open again. I have a great desire to do that now,
and Freud agrees. It was closed for a time because of difficulties with
the authorities. But everything will be in order soon enough.

Yes, there is certainly much that is beautiful about the Jesus legend.
Isn't the reason that the New Testament is written in Greek because
in the early Middle Ages the written language was exclusively Greek,
and Latin came only later? The monastic scribes never made use of
the vernacular [*Volkssprache*] and therefore not of Hebrew either. – The
fact that people connect their tendency for cruelty with the beautiful

---

21 Ludwig Wüllner (1858–1938) was a German concert and operatic tenor.

teachings of Jesus is understandable when we accept that the Jesus legend is a popular myth [*Volksmythos*]. The attitude of humanity is ambivalent; hatred and revenge and cruelty live on in the unconscious side-by-side with higher moral and ethical feelings. Jesus was a very special person, but with all the fundamental human tendencies united within him, simply a person. And so it was with his followers. – Of course the German question is a powerful point here, since we are a German country. How will that end? . . .

Sunday, January 28, 1923. . . . I will get a patient this week; Dr. Hitschmann will send her to me, to my apartment because I do not have official consent from the Ambulatorium.

Vienna, February 2, 1923. I now have a very pleasant friendship with Mrs. Blumgart,[22] an American. She is a likable and nice person; naturally we have so many interests in common. . . . My first Viennese patient did not come at the appointed time. Not a good beginning. Luckily, Hitschmann and Freud told me that this happens fairly often.

Jeanne worried about political developments in Germany. She underplayed the anti-Semitic riots in Vienna when she wrote to her parents, presumably in order not to upset them or herself, but she also wrote, "actually very interesting to experience." However, she mentioned her "confusion" and amazement that the public apparently "remained so quiet."

She also wrote about her enthusiasm at starting her psychiatric training under Julius Wagner-Jauregg, which was a compulsory part of her training.

Vienna, February 5, 1923. . . . How horrible the situation in Germany is.[23] The insane hatred and the craziness in the world can sometimes overwhelm one like a nightmare. There was an anti-Jewish demonstration here again yesterday, where I happened to be. Magnus Hirschfeld,[24] from Berlin, was giving a lecture at the Konzerthaus. He is a sexual pathologist and talked about the pathology of love life. Very popular but scientific and good. After half an hour all of a sudden whistling, screaming, tumult, stink bombs, shootings, and scuffles. I was astounded that the public largely remained so quiet, but of course there was also confusion. It was nothing but an anti-Semitic demonstration. Strange and actually very interesting to experience.

22 Ruth Mack Brunswick. Blumgart was her married name at the time.
23 At the time Germany was in the throes of hyperinflation. In addition, France had occupied the Ruhr region in order to force Germany to pay reparations from World War I.
24 Magnus Hirschfeld (1868–1935) was an early advocate of homosexual rights. In 1919 he founded the Institute of Sex Research, in Berlin. A frequent target of right-wing and Nazi violence, he was forced to leave Germany in 1933.

Of course the perpetrators got away and only a couple of younger fellows were arrested. What all can't happen in the good City of Vienna; actually it was much ado about nothing, but it really did stink. I was with M., and at the end got together with Dr. Catz and his family. We went to a coffeehouse and had an analytic discussion about it . . .. He is a Jungian, a strange sort, but I think a good person, intelligent and it was very interesting to talk with him. Except that he has no idea what analysis is. Of course, he often achieves good results with his psychotherapy, but why do such people have to call themselves analysts, while being completely blind to any analytic understanding? The more one penetrates analytic science, the more one realizes how difficult this terrain is, how little one's previous book-learning means, and how absolutely necessary a thorough self-analysis is (in the *true* analytical sense) if one is to come to some understanding of the human soul. I think I told you last summer that when I began my analysis, Freud once told me laughingly, "But you already know everything!" And in fact I did know a few things about theory, but now I recognize the difference between knowing and knowing, and the inestimable value of experiencing it oneself. Of course it is also an inestimable advantage to go through a training period with someone like Freud, . . . who with clarity stands above all morality and all prejudice. But it takes time to appreciate that to its full extent as well. It is strange to have a session before a Society meeting, where discussions sometimes become heated. Everyone is actually waiting for Freud to say something, and what he says is always important and simple and clear, in contrast to the often hopeless confusion of many of the others.

Did I already tell you that I will start work tomorrow at Wagner-Jauregg's psychiatric clinic? I'm very excited to see how things will go there. Wagner has a very cynical attitude toward analysis, but he gives free rein to Schilder, his first assistant, who works analytically. I have to look around at first and see how it works. My first patient from the polyclinic didn't show up; I'm now awaiting another one and will be busy enough. But I have a great desire to work and have the feeling that a large quantity of energy has been released that I must use in some form. . . . Farewell, hugs with two extra birthday kisses from your Jeanne.

The following letter shows how Jeanne and Freud's relationship became increasingly collegial and friendly. From this point on she called him "Prof. Freud," perhaps distancing herself somewhat from her parents. He asked her to have 25 florin (the exact cost of an analysis session) transferred as a gift in honor of Prof. Jelgersma on the occasion of his silver anniversary. This was actually a request to her father – a curious intervention on Freud's part.

Jeanne gave Freud roses – "Christmas roses," but roses in name, nonetheless. It is doubtful that she informed her parents of the two supervised cases that she undertook. Regarding her own analysis, she told them that there was still "a lot" to be done, but that she was almost at the end.

This was also when she became friends with Anna Freud, with whom she felt she had much in common.

Vienna, April 7, 1923. Dear Mother and Father, first a request from Prof. Freud. He received a circular letter in honor of Jelgersma on his 25 years of professorship. Now he is to be honored with a painted portrait, and people are collecting money. Because it is difficult for Freud to transfer Dutch money to Holland, I offered to ask Father to pay it with a postal check. Vadertje,[25] could you send the 25 florin? Freud will then subtract it from the next fee invoice, and write to Dr. de Vries that his contribution will be coming from you. I am enclosing the postal check. That would just be a small effort for you, or? Many thanks in advance.

Of course you've already heard about my trip to Salzburg. The two days on the lake at St. Wolfgang were lovely, the snowy mountains magnificent, wild and capricious, shining sun, and so many flowers. I brought back a lot of Christmas roses, magnificently large, and brought one to Freud, who was also charmed.

My patient is doing well for now. That is, therapeutically there is of course no telling yet. Since starting treatment the man is feeling much better, but that doesn't mean anything. He's doing that only to be pleasing; the difficulties are yet to come. After about a week he told me that at the beginning he recoiled somewhat from treatment by a female doctor, but that he had found it easy and it actually wasn't hard for him to talk about intimate matters. So, thankfully a considerable transference. He is a laborer from a completely normal, impoverished proletarian family, but he has read much and is so developed that I can learn a lot from him. That is very pleasant, and as a result I feel inspired to work, and he has so much insight. The girl is much less intelligent, but I can't say where that will go either. In any case, the work is inspiring, though hard.

There is a lot still to be done in my own analysis, but thankfully the greatest difficulties are now behind me. The contours are all finished, only the details and finishing touches are missing. Luckily, both of us want to do the thing thoroughly; I am very grateful to Prof. Freud for that. I am sure that it would give me no peace otherwise, and that I would have to battle new problems repeatedly. It's going slowly, but it is solid as a result. Anna Freud visited me yesterday, very pleasant. She is dear and refined and very competent. I think that we will get along well with each other. She has also begun to conduct analyses

25 The Dutch diminutive of Father.

herself, with an 11-year-old child and a young girl. She is so pleasantly simple and normal, actually quite un-Viennese.

In the following letter, Jeanne again felt it necessary to defend herself and Freud against her father's obvious growing distrust and impatience about the financial arrangements. She pleaded with him and discussed Freud's personal situation as well:

Vienna, April 12, 1923. Dear Father and Mother, I have before me your two letters dated the 7th that are begging for a response. First, of course, to Father's somewhat biting remark about Prof. Freud, as it weighs most heavily upon me. Well, Vadertje. Your notion that he will be happy to see me again after the vacation is completely unfounded. I happen to know, and not only from him, that he has a permanent list of inquiries from analysts and patients in America that he is unable to accept because he has no time. And Americans pay 1½ times more than I do: $15. That is because the cost of living in America is much greater than here in Europe and, for example, the most prestigious analysts in America (Brill, among others), ask $20 to $25. It's actually ridiculous that Prof. Freud gets less, but he is unable to command these enormous fees. In England, Jones (the first analyst there) gets exactly as much as Prof. Freud. It's clear that his requirements are not excessive. And as far as I am concerned, if money were his primary concern he would send me away, and take an American who pays 1½ times more.

You are correct that Prof. Freud considers me a good object of study. But that is his right. What is important to me is that I be a good object of study for myself; who better to learn about than oneself under such excellent guidance? So much as concerns the analyst in me. What value analysis has and will have for my personal happiness is of course more difficult for me to convey to you, because you would have to know the analysis yourself. You will only see the effects of it in the future. I cannot give you proof of its positive effects; at present I have only my subjective interpretation to go by, and I do not know to what extent I can use that to get you to understand. I am convinced that analysis will have a major influence on my life, and make me more open, free, and happy, and more able to work. The future will tell whether I'm right. It goes without saying that I am grateful to Prof. Freud, and actually in two respects. First because analysis is his creation and without him (at least now) it would not exist; and second, not only is Freud an analyst, he is a fine, intellectually elevated, and thoroughly healthy person. As a result, dealing with him is a great privilege and joy. He is a person from whom one can learn much, and that is really a priceless privilege and pleasure.

Recently a particularly discriminating physician told me that one thing is certain, namely that Freud is the greatest figure to emerge from the medical profession in the past 50 years. It is not to humanity's credit that such a man should have to fight for his material existence into his 61st year (1918) without a cent in assets (while supporting a family of six children, who have all become competent people, in addition to an elderly mother, two sisters, and other assorted family members). But it's always the case that humanity doesn't bother much with its great men, and perhaps that's not so bad. But it is surely not unjust that such a man should earn greatly during the final years of his life. . . . But actually I'm most pleased with the first argument, that he could accept another analysand in my place and earn 1½ times more. That alone refutes your insinuations.

What Mother writes is closer to the truth: Prof. Freud is interested in me and expects something of me, and so in this respect he prefers working with me than with others whom he may find less appealing. But the fact that the dissemination of his life work is not more important to him than my happiness is demonstrated by what he said to me a few days ago: "Actually, you could decide after the conclusion of analysis whether you wish to become an analyst or choose something different." I was astonished because for me the matter is settled; I also know that he considers me to be well suited, and as I already wrote, he absolutely expects something of me. It was merely his intention to point out that I must be completely free to find my own path. He told me once, "If you were to tell me that you don't want to become an analyst or want to work as an analyst only for a few years, I'd be just as interested in you." As mother writes, that's wonderful for me. And now on to the other points that you touched on. This is becoming a lengthy epistle! I promise you that I will be as careful as I can with the menfolk. I don't think that the peril is great, so long as one looks around carefully and uses one's reason. In addition, in Prof. Freud I have a pleasant and trusted advisor. . . . I went to see *Don Juan* yesterday, a fantastic performance which I enjoyed deeply. I think it is the most beautiful opera I know of. Dr. Deutsch gave me a seat in the loge. He wasn't able to go, so I attended with Anna Freud, Dr. Rank, and Dr. Storfer, all analysts, very convivial. . . . Greetings to both of you and hugs from your Jeanne.

[Marginal note:] Vadertje, in the final analysis I am very grateful to you for letting me be free, and for trusting me to choose the proper path. I myself have no doubts, and that's saying quite a lot.

Freud also asked her for financial assistance for his ex-patient, undoubtedly the Wolf-Man:

Vienna, Wednesday, April 18, 1923. . . . Prof. Freud is currently collecting money for an ex-patient of his. He was a severe neurotic who was completely cured and became a worthy person. Unfortunately, his circumstances are so terrible that he is almost starving. He's a Russian, at one time he was fabulously wealthy, but lost everything in the war and is unable to return to Bolshevist Russia. He lives in Vienna, but as a foreigner can't get an emigration permit. He is intermittently employed, but for hunger wages, and in addition he has a sick wife. After Freud he has not been lacking in energy, but there is really no work, not for the Viennese, and much less for foreigners. I would like to give him 100 florin; Father, do you think that is all right? And would you send me 300 florin next month?

In her next letter, Jeanne reported that Freud had had surgery that appeared to have been minor. She shared her concerns and doubts with her colleague Ruth, and with his daughter Anna:

Vienna, April 26, 1923. . . . Many thanks for the money, Vadertje, and for the 100 florin for Prof. Freud's patient. Last week was one of terrible anxiety, I mean regarding Prof. Freud himself. On Saturday he had a small growth in his mouth surgically removed. It appears to have been benign and of little concern. Now we are all fearful for this old man; our first thought, of course, was cancer. I do not know for certain what it was. However, the surgery was more extensive than anticipated, and a fairly large piece of mucosa was excised. Now of course it is always possible that the entire growth has been removed by thorough and timely surgery, even if it was cancer. But some concern remains. Prof. Freud imagined that he would be able to return to work on Saturday afternoon or otherwise on Monday, but he won't until next Monday. He had to stay in the clinic for two days, bled, and suffered terrible pain, in addition to which he is exhausted and weak. He's upset that he can't immediately continue as he had before. Thank goodness he's getting better day by day, and we hope for the best. Ruth and I comforted each other in our anxiety. It's so disconcerting to go for more than a week without analysis! Anna (his daughter) spent two days and nights with him in the clinic; she's also exhausted, as you can imagine. But yesterday she was beaming with happiness that things were going so much better. It would probably be best for you not to discuss this with others. And if anybody asks about it, tell them it was something minor and unimportant. After all, it's so bothersome when there is a lot of serious talk right away. Immediately, someone like Freud is thought to be dead, or something similar. Imagine, during the war American newspapers reported three times that he had committed suicide and was in his grave! If people hear the word cancer nowadays, he might as well already be dead and buried by tomorrow. And yet it is very possible that it really was a benign growth. I am writing to you about this because I am so distressed. I saw Prof. Freud briefly yesterday and all of a sudden he seemed so very old.

It must have been a considerable shock for her when she received a letter from her mother and learned that her father had suddenly taken ill. It seems that she had earlier had experience with his episodes of pain because she simply wrote about the nervous states that supposedly played a large role. Or was she perhaps trying to reassure him and herself? Freud was giving her no peace either:

> Vienna, April 30, 1923. Dear Mother, you write in letter 53 about Father as if I knew of his recurrent illness. A letter must have gotten lost, because I know nothing about this new episode of pain. It's a good thing that van Weelie found nothing; what caused the pain was probably a constriction of blood vessels and irritation of the nerves as a result of localized ischemia, leading to pain. My presumption is that something psychic is causing this constriction of the blood vessels, worries, difficulties, aversion, in any case. Aging, and the mild calcification of the blood vessels associated with it then lead to such a state and facilitate an organic reaction. But nervous states generally play the greatest role in such matters. The fact that other physicians are not deaf to this possibility is shown by van Weelie's recommendation that he not let himself get upset by worldly matters. His advice, that he travel, is excellent!! . . . Prof. Freud began work again this morning, and says that he is feeling quite good. . . . Warm greetings and kisses, Jeanne.

The correspondence in the Berkovits-Lampl archive ends on this note.

Afterword

Deciphering Sigmund Freud's letters to one of his most promising students, and later colleague, Jeanne Lampl-de Groot, was a fascinating experience, as it put me in touch in a uniquely personal way with that period in the interwar years when history hung in the balance. Behind the appearance of normalcy, and although the work on psychoanalytic theory and practice continued, one can sense the progressive constriction of life as Europe slid into the abyss.

As a young person, Jeanne de Groot led a relatively privileged life. Her family was able to finance a five-month stay in Italy from late September 1921 to mid-February 1922; for her it was a welcome escape from depression, a grieving mother, and the lock-down necessitated by the war. From Italy, Jeanne, now a medical doctor, wrote to Freud asking him to train her in psychoanalysis. Freud had already made a name for himself with his theories of the unconscious, so her request, out of the blue, was more than a little daring and revealed an adventuresome spirit.

Both Freud and de Groot were exceptionally gifted letter writers, able to express intimate feelings of closeness, personal and professional criticism, their awareness of what was unfolding, and, of course, gossip. The two bodies of letters presented here open a window onto the social history of the times and add inside details to our understanding of anti-Semitism and the forces that led to migration.

Freud's letters to Jeanne contain a mixture of day-to-day details – some trivial, some weighty – about his children and grandchildren, a surprising openness about money, his own uncertainties regarding aspects of psychoanalytic theory, and his willingness to entertain that someone else – such as Jeanne – might have greater insight, especially into female sexuality and psychology. He also shared with her his battle with jaw cancer and his seemingly endless and excruciating surgeries and prosthetic fittings – often with an almost bemused sense of distance. And, of course, cigars were a frequent topic, not just the enjoyment thereof but in terms of their availability and even their use as an ersatz currency.

DOI: 10.4324/9781003268130-5

It is a terrible loss, however, that Jeanne decided to have Anna Freud destroy her half of the correspondence. We do not know why she made that request, nor, really, why Anna complied with it. There are several areas where having both sides of the correspondence would have been helpful. For one thing, from Freud's responses and advice we cannot derive a clear picture of what was going on with Hans Lampl, Jeanne's husband. But from them it is evident that Jeanne must have written lengthy descriptions of his moods and behaviors that might have given us insight into the dynamics of their relationship and into the nature of her relationship with Freud. And so we can only venture guesses.

Perhaps even more importantly, we do not have a record of her conversations with Freud about what he referred to as her "first intellectual offspring," her 1927 paper "The Evolution of the Oedipus Complex in Women." It is likely that she rehearsed lines of reasoning with him, which would have given us a greater sense of her development as a psychoanalytic thinker in her own right.

None of this, however, diminishes the importance of the letters we have, which testify to the vibrant relationship that existed between the two. And Jeanne expressed much of her excitement about Freud and his ideas in her letters to her parents.

Jeanne Lampl-de Groot guarded her trove of letters from Freud throughout her time in Vienna and Berlin, and then – in Amsterdam – through the five-year duration of WWII. For more than 40 years after the war, she kept them safely locked up in her home in a small cupboard next to the analytic couch and chimney, hidden behind several bottles of the Dutch gin that had been a major source of the de Groot family's prosperity.

In my work on these letters, I was inspired by Ilse Grubrich-Simitis' *Back to Freud's Texts; Making Silent Documents Speak*,[1] and Gerhard Fichtner's regular column on "Freud as a letter-writer" in the German-language *Jahrbuch der Psychoanalyse*. Through them I came to understand the importance of preserving Freud's writings, as they offer an intimate view into his developing thoughts and theories, his organizational talents, his perspective on the arts and culture, above all his rich language.

This book would never have seen the light of day without Edith and Robert Berkovits-Lampl's generosity. I am also indebted to Gerhard Fichtner and Albrecht Hirschmüller for their practical textual advice; Joachim Danckwardt for his help in correcting my German translations of Jeanne's Dutch letters to her parents and help with the bibliographical notes; and to the publishers of the German edition, Hans-Jürgen Wirth and Johann Wirth, and the German proofreader Laura Huber.

---

1   Grubrich-Simitis, I. (1993). *Zurück zu Freuds Texten. Stumme Dokumente sprechen machen.* Frankfurt a.M.; Fischer.

I am grateful for the assistance of many others, of whom I will mention here my colleague Kerry Kelly Novick for finding my inspiring English translator, Kenneth Kronenberg. I thank my editor Susannah Frearson at Routledge and my colleagues at the International Psychoanalytic Association, Rhoda Bawdekar and Gabriela Legorreta, Chair of the IPA Publications Committee, who waited patiently while personal circumstances delayed my work on the English edition for more than a year, and Valérie Bouville, President of the German Psychoanalytical Association, for mediating the financial support.

For the original Dutch edition, I thank my dedicated publisher Elsbeth Greven,[2] the linguist Frida Balk-Smit Duyzentkunst, and the Dutch poet Tobias Reinders, who endured many dull moments while I was working on this project. And finally, I am especially indebted to his mother, my life partner Etty Mulder, musicologist and cultural historian. This work is dedicated to her cherished memory.

Gertie Bögels, Maarn, 2022

2 Greven, E. (2009). "Hundert Jahre Freud-Ausgaben in den Niederlanden." *Luzifer-Amor*, 22, 54–70.

Literature

Bentinck van Schoonheten, A. (2016). *Karl Abraham: Life and Work, a Biography*. London: Karnac, pp. xxiii, 432.

Bernfeld, S. & Cassirer Bernfeld, S. (1944). "Freud's Early Childhood." *Bulletin of the Menninger Clinic*, VIII, 107–115.

Brinkgreve, C. (1984). *Psychoanalyse in Nederland. Een vestigingsstrijd*. Amsterdam: De Arbeiderspers.

Bulhof, I. (1983). *Freud en Nederland. De interpretatie en invloed van zijn ideeën*. Baarn: Ambo.

Davies, K. & Fichtner, G. (2006). *Freud's Library. A Comprehensive Catalogue/Freuds Bibliothek. Vollständiger Katalog*. London: The Freud Museum. London/Tübingen: edition diskord.

Fichtner, G. (2004). ". . . für den sein Elend geniessenden Dulder." *Jahrbuch Psychoanalyse*, 49, 170–175.

———. (2008). "'. . . ein Stück kleines Emigrantenelend neben dem großen.' Ein Brief Freuds an Jeanne Lampl-de Groot aus dem Jahre 1938." In C. Frank, L. Hermann & H. Hinz (eds.), *Jahrbuch der Psychoanalyse*, vol. 57. Stuttgart: frommann-holzboog, pp. 201–213.

Freud, A. (1928). *Introduction to the Technique of Child Analysis*. New York: Ayer.

———. (1966–1980). *The Writings of Anna Freud* (in 8 vols.). New York: International Universities Press.

Freud, H.C. (2011). *Electra vs Oedipus. The Drama of the Mother-Daughter Relationship*. London/New York: Routledge.

Freud, S. (1900). "The Interpretation of Dreams." In *The Standard Edition of the Complete Psychological Works of Sigmund Freud*, vols. IV and V. London: Hogarth.

———. (1914). "The Moses of Michelangelo." In *The Standard Edition*, vol. XII, p. 233.

———. (1916–17a, 1963). "Introductory Lectures on Psycho-Analysis." In *The Standard Edition*, vol. XV. London: Hogarth, p. 193.

———. (1920). "Beyond the Pleasure Principle." In *The Standard Edition*, vol. XIII, p. 60.

———. (1925). "An Autobiographical Study." In *The Standard Edition*, vol. XX, pp. 7–70.

———. (1926). "The Question of Lay Analysis: Conversations with an Impartial Person." In *The Standard Edition*, vol. XX, pp. 183–250.

———. (1931). "Female Sexuality." In *The Standard Edition*, vol. XXI, pp. 226–227, 241.

———. (1932). "The Acquisition and Control of Fire." In *The Standard Edition*, vol. XXII, pp. 187–193.

———. (1933a). "New Introductory Lectures on Psychoanalysis." In *The Standard Edition*, vol. XXII, pp. 7–30, 31–56, 57–80, 81–111, 112–135, 158–182.

———. (1933b [1932]). "Why War?" In *The Standard Edition*, vol. XXII. London: Hogarth, pp. 197–215.

———. (1935). "'Postscript' to the 'Autobiographical Study'." In *The Standard Edition*, vol. XX, pp. 71–74.

———. (1960). *Briefe 1873–1939*. Selected and edited by Ernst and Lucie Freud. Frankfurt a.M.: Fischer.

———. (2011). "Sigmund Freud, Martha Bernays." In G. Fichtner, I. Grubrich-Simitis & A. Hirschmüller (eds.), *Die Brautbriefe 1882–1886*, vol. 1. "Sei mein, wie ich mir's denke". Frankfurt a.M.: Fischer.

Freud, S. & Eitingon, M. (2004). *Briefwechsel 1906–1939*. Michael Schröter (ed.). Tübingen: edition diskord.

Frijling-Schreuder, E.C.M. (1987). "In Memoriam dr. J.A. Lampl-de Groot." *Maandblad Geestelijke Volksgezondheid*, 9(87), 971–978.

Gardiner, M. (ed.). (1971). *The Wolf-Man, by the Wolf-Man: With "The Case of the Wolf-Man"*. New York: Basic Books.

Greven, E. (2009). "Hundert Jahre Freud-Ausgaben in den Niederlanden." *Luzifer-Amor*, 22, 54–70.

Groen-Prakken, H. & Ladan, A. (eds.). (1993). *The Dutch Annual of Psychoanalysis 1993*, vol. I. Amsterdam: Swets & Zeitlinger.

Grubrich-Simitis, I. (1993). *Zurück zu Freuds Texten. Stumme Dokumente sprechen machen*. Frankfurt a.M.: Fischer.

Horkheimer, M. (1995). *Gesammelte Schriften* (vols. 15–17). Frankfurt a.M.: Fischer.

Jones, E. (1957). *The Life and Work of Sigmund Freud*, vol. 3. New York: Basic Books.

Kedde, B. (1972). *Herinneringen aan een groot Schiedammer*. Schiedam: Drukkerij de Eendracht.

King, P. & Steiner, R. (eds.). (1991). *The Freud-Klein Controversies 1941–45*. London/New York: Routledge.

Klein, E. (1951). "Johan H.W. van Ophuijsen." *International Journal of Psycho-Analysis*, 32, 134–135.

Lampl-de Groot, J. (1927). "Zur Entwicklung des Oedipuskomplexes der Frau." *Internationale Zeitschrift für Psychoanalyse*, 13, 269–282.

———. (1933). "Problems of Femininity." *Psychoanalytic Quarterly*, 2, 489–518.

———. (1956). "Anmerkungen zur psychoanalytischen Triebtheorie." In *Psyche – Z. Psychoanalyse*, 10, 194–204.

———. (1965). *The Development of the Mind. Psychoanalytic Papers on Clinical and Theoretical Problems*. New York: International Universities Press.

———. (1985). *Man and Mind. Collected Papers of Jeanne Lampl-de Groot*. New York: International Universities Press and Assen: Van Gorkum.

———. (1993). *Over vrouwelijke seksualiteit*. Tonja Kivits (ed.), Tinke Davids (trans.). Amsterdam: Boom.

Landauer, K. (1991). *Theorie der Affekte und andere Schriften zur Ich-Organisation*. H.-J. Rothe (ed.). Frankfurt a.M.: Fischer.

Mann, T. (1933). *Past Masters and Other Papers*. New York: Knopf.

———. (1974). *Gesammelte Werke*. Frankfurt a.M.: Fischer.

Meijer, M. (2011). *M. Vasalis. Een biografie*. Amsterdam: Van Oorschot.

Montessori, M. (1960). "Dr. Hans Lampl – 1889–1958." *The International Journal of Psychology*, 4, 163–164.

Multatuli (Pseudonym of Eduard Douwes Dekker). (1995). *Volledige werken* (25 vols.). Amsterdam: G.A. van Oorschot.

Pam, M. & Sijmons, R. (1977). "Psychoanalyse. Jeanne Lampl-de Groot heeft nog bij Freud op de divan gelegen." *Vrij Nederland*, 38, 57.

Rothe, H-J. (ed.). (1991). *Karl Landauer: Theorie der Affekte und andere Schriften zur Ich-Organisation*. Frankfurt a.M.: Fischer.

Roudinesco, E. & Plon, M. (2004). *Wörterbuch der Psychoanalyse. Namen, Länder, Werke, Begriffe*. Vienna: Springer.

Spanjaard, J. & Mekking, R. (1976). "Psychoanalyse in den Niederlanden." In D. Eicke (ed.), *Die Psychologie des 20. Jahrhunderts*, vol. III. Zürich: Kindler, pp. 55–72.

Stouten, H. (2011). *Marie Bonaparte 1882–1962. Freuds prinses zoekt haar dode moeder*. Amsterdam: Amsterdam University Press.

Stroeken, H. (2009). "Johan van Ophuijsen, Padang/Indonesien 1882 – New York 1950." *Luzifer Amor*, 22, 7–44.

Szecsödy, I. (2007). "Sándor, Ferenczi – the First Intersubjectivist." *The Scandinavian Psychoanalytic Review*, 30, 33–42.

van der Leeuw, P.J., Frijling-Schreuder, E.C.M. & Kuiper, P.C. (eds.). (1967). *Hoofdstukken uit de hedendaagse psychoanalyse*. Arnhem: Van Loghum Slaterus.

van Lieburg, M.J. (1995). "J.A. Lampl de-Groot (1895–1987)." *Medisch Contact*, 50(45), 1427.

Wallinga, J. (1987). 'In memoriam Jeanne A. Lampl-de Groot', *Jahrbuch der Psychoanalyse, 21, p. 7–13. Stuttgart: Frommann-Holzboog, 1987*.

Young-Bruehl, E. (1988). *Anna Freud: A Biography*. New York: Summit Books.

Works by Jeanne Lampl-de Groot

Arlow, J.A., Freud, A., Lampl-de Groot, J. & Beres, D. (1968). "Panel Discussion." *International Journal of Psychoanalysis*, 49, 506–512.

Lampl-de Groot, J. (1928). "The Evolution of the Oedipus Complex in Women." International Journal of Psychoanalysis, 9, 332–345.

Lampl-de Groot, J. (1932). "Zu den Problemen der Weiblichkeit." *Int. Zeitschrift für Psychoanalyse*, 19, 385–415.

———. (1933). "Problems of Femininity." *Psychoanalytic Quarterly*, 2, 489–518.

———. (1939). "Considerations of Methodology in Relation to the Psychology of Small Children." *International Journal of Psychoanalysis*, 20, 408–417.

———. (1946). "The Pre-Oedipal Phase in the Development of the Male Child." *Psychoanalytic Study of the Child*, 2, 75–83.

———. (1947). "On the Development of the Ego and Super-Ego." *International Journal of Psychoanalysis*, 28, 7–11.

———. (1950). "On Masturbation and its Influence on General Development." *Psychoanalytic Study of the Child*, 5, 153–174.

———. (1952). "Re-Evaluation of the Role of the Oedipus Complex." *International Journal of Psychoanalysis*, 33, 335–342.

———. (1954). "Problems of Psycho-Analytic Training." *International Journal of Psychoanalysis*, 35, 184–187.

———. (1956a). "The Role of Identification in Psycho-Analytic Procedure." *International Journal of Psychoanalysis*, 37, 456–459.

———. (1956b). "The Theory of Instinctual Drives." *International Journal of Psychoanalysis*, 37, 354–359.

———. (1956c). "Anmerkungen zur psychoanalytischen Triebtheorie." *Psyche – Z. Psychoanalyse*, 10, 194–204.

———. (1957). "On Defense and Development: Normal and Pathological." *Psychoanalytic Study of the Child*, 12, 114–126.

———. (1959). "Psycho-Analysis and its Relation to Certain Other Fields of Natural Science." *International Journal of Psychoanalysis*, 40, 169–179.

———. (1960a). "On Adolescence." *Psychoanalytic Study of the Child*, 15, 95–103.

———. (1960b). "Depression und Aggression." In K. Draeger, H.-E. Richter, G. Scheunert & G. Seeger (eds.), *Jahrbuch der Psychoanalyse*, vol. I. Cologne: Westdeutscher Verlag, pp. 145–160.

———. (1962a). "Ego Ideal and Superego." *Psychoanalytic Study of the Child*, 17, 94–106.

———. (1962b). "Zur Behandlungstechnik bei neurotischen Patientinnen: Einige Bemerkungen zu den Beiträgen von P.C. Kuiper und M. Mitscherlich." *Psyche – Z. Psychoanalyse*, 15, 681–683.

———. (1963a). "Symptom Formation and Character Formation." *International Journal of Psychoanalysis*, 44, 1–11. "Symptombildung und Charakterbildung." *Psyche – Z. Psychoanalyse*, 17, 1–22.

———. (1963b). "Ich-Ideal und Über-Ich." *Psyche – Z. Psychoanalyse*, 17, 321–332.

———. (1964a). "Remarks on Genesis, Structuralization, and Functioning of the Mind." *Psychoanalytic Study of the Child*, 19, 48–57.

———. (1964b). "Heinz Hartmanns Beiträge zur Psychoanalyse." *Psyche – Z Psychoanal.*, 18, 321–329.

———. (1965). "Zur Entwicklungsgeschichte des Ödipuskomplexes der Frau." *Psyche – Z. Psychoanalyse*, 19, 403–416.

———. (1967a). "On Obstacles Standing in the Way of Psychoanalytic Cure." *Psychoanalytic Study of the Child*, 22, 20–35.

———. (1967b). "Die Zusammenarbeit von Patient und Analytiker in der Psychoanalytischen Behandlung: Übertragung, Gegenübertragung, Einfühlung und Intuition." *Psyche – Z. Psychoanalyse*, 21, 73–83.

———. (1968). "Gedanken über Vorteile und Gefahren der 'Einsichkeit' in der wissenschaftlichen Forschung." *Psyche – Z. Psychoanalyse*, 22, 672–678.

———. (1969a). "Reflections on the Development of Psychoanalysis: Technical Implications in Analytic Treatment." *International Journal of Psychoanalysis*, 50, 567–572.

———. (1969b). "Introduction to the Scientific Programme of the 26th Congress of the International Psycho-Analytical Association, Rome (27 July 1969 to 1 August inclusive)." *International Journal of Psychoanalysis*, 50, 3–4.

———. (1972). *Schwierigkeiten der Psychoanalyse in Vergangenheit und Gegenwart.* Frankfurt a.M.: Fischer.

———. (1975). "Vicissitudes of Narcissism and Problems of Civilization." *Psychoanalytic Study of the Child*, 30, 663–681.

———. (1976a). "Mourning in a 6-Year-Old Girl." *Psychoanalytic Study of the Child*, 31, 273–281.

———. (1976b). "Personal Experience with Psychoanalytic Technique and Theory During the Last Half Century." *Psychoanalytic Study of the Child*, 31, 283–296.

———. (1981). "Notes on 'Multiple Personality'." *Psychoanalytic Quarterly*, 50, 614–624.

———. (1982). "Thoughts on Psychoanalytic Views of Female Psychology 1927–1977." *Psychoanalytic Quarterly*, 51, 1–18.

———. (1983). "On the Process of Mourning." *Psychoanalytic Study of the Child*, 38, 9–13.

———. (1985). *Man and Mind. Collected Papers of Jeanne Lampl-de Groot.* New York: International Universities Press, pp. 12–32.

Name Index

Subject Index

.

For Product Safety Concerns and Information please contact our EU
representative GPSR@taylorandfrancis.com
Taylor & Francis Verlag GmbH, Kaufingerstraße 24, 80331 München, Germany

9 781032 213811